VITEX
AGNUS-CASTUS
LATIFOLIA

SPIRAEA
X BUMALDA
whatever

GREPIS
on fence

boulders

LONICERA
TATARICA

SANGUINARIA
CANADENSIS
groundcover

STROB.

PENDULA
RUBRA

ALTHEA

JUNIPERUS

ILEX
GLABRA

POLYGONATUM

LUNARIA

POLYG.

LUPINUS

BOLT.

BAPTISIA

GILLENIA

IS ENSATA
SHADOW

BUXUS

POLYG.

BUXUS

CRAMBE

ASTER

BAPTISIA

MALVA

boulder

STILBE
CANAL

ACHILLEA

LIATRIS

SIDALCEA

LYCHNIS

ASTER FRIK

boulder

VALERIANA

PHALARIS

LILIUM

SALVIA
SCLAREA

SEDUM

PLATY

ALLIUM

CHRYS.

PHYS.

COSMOS

ASTILBE
'BRIDAL VEIL'

SEDUM
A.J.

NEP.

STEPH

PIANTHUS

ALCH

ACHILLEA

PET.

SEDUM

PETUNIA

HERTA

BERBERIS

BERBERIS

American Border Gardens

American Border Gardens

MELANIE FLEISCHMANN

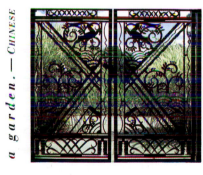

If you would

be happy all

your life, plant

a garden. —CHINESE

Photographs by KAREN HALVERSON
Illustrations by RANDY HARELSON
Design by ALICE COOKE

CLARKSON POTTER/PUBLISHERS NEW YORK

Photographs copyright © 1993 by Karen Halverson

Photographs on pages 3, 5, 6, 8, 13 (right), 14 (left), 23, 25, 26, 27, 30, 32, 33, 35, 37, 38 (bottom), 39(bottom), 74, 103, 105, 118, 120, 123, and 134 were taken by Melanie Fleischmann.

Copyright © 1993 by Melanie Fleischmann

Published by Clarkson N. Potter, Inc., 201 East 50th Street, New York, New York 10022.
Member of the Crown Publishing Group.

CLARKSON N. POTTER, POTTER and colophon are trademarks of Clarkson N. Potter, Inc.

Manufactured in Japan

Design by Alice Cooke

Library of Congress Cataloging-in-Publication Data

Fleischmann, Melanie.
American border gardens / by Melanie Fleischmann; photographs by Karen Halverson; design by Alice Cooke.
Includes index.
1. Garden borders—United States. 2. Garden borders—United States—Pictorial works. I. Title.
SB424.F57 1992 716—dc20 91-19175 CIP

ISBN 0-517-57646-5

10 9 8 7 6 5 4 3 2 1

First Edition

For my husband, for whom the sun is always shining, and
for my daughters, two of the most delightful ways in the world to
convert a working day into a working minute

Acknowledgments

To Lee Bailey, who started this, and provided spiritual sunshine; Deborah Geltman,
one great agent, who I'm now convinced would tackle anything;
Alexandra Enders, who did for this book what a gardener has to do for a border: plan,
cajole, wait, and edit, with considerable skill and grace; Jane Clark, for my
first border, among other forms of encouragement; Alice Cooke, for creating such a
beautiful package for this book; Karen Halverson, for momentarily leaving
the world of art galleries in order to work on a book; Randy Harelson for his lovely
drawings and endlessly cheerful outlook; all the borders' owners and keepers,
who led me through their gardens and were generous with their knowledge;
and last, all at Clarkson Potter, especially
Howard Klein and Lauren Shakely: thank you.

Contents

Preface

My first attempt at making a flower border was when I was about fifteen. My family lived in rural South Carolina and there wasn't a nursery within fifty miles, so I plowed through my mother's considerable collection of catalogs. I believed that anything that would grow in Michigan would grow in South Carolina, only better, and I ordered my plants accordingly.

The result was an appalling collection of plants in teardrop-shaped beds that might have been appropriate in the formal parterres of Versailles but looked pretty silly in the middle of a hot, sandy field, closely scrutinized by alligators. The plants had the good sense to wilt away, and my mother had the grace not to say anything at all.

My next attempt was some ten years later, on a large terrace sixteen stories above the streets of Manhattan. The little design experience I had had at that point was in the realm of interiors, and my instinct was to treat my plants like tables and chairs. When I found a grouping imperfect, I simply heaved planters and tubs around until the arrangement was more pleasing. I had climbing roses so exuberant that they made appearances in the apartment above mine, clematis that nearly collapsed a substantial bower, and delphiniums as hardy as daisies — and daisies, too, plus sweet peas, lilies, hollyhocks, and phlox, and a lavender bush the size of a large armchair. I read quantities of literature about the complexities of growing these plants, and couldn't understand what all the fuss was about, because I did little more than provide water and, when I remembered, plant food.

Of course, the sterilized potting soil that I brought up by the bagful was the horticultural equivalent of rocket fuel. I could also fine-tune it to suit each plant perfectly, giving my lavender the sandy alkaline soil it loves, and planting my Siberian irises in the heavier soil they prefer. My soil had no weed seeds, and sixteen stories in the air, few blew in. So I had no inkling of what it really meant to wage war with weeds.

Ken Druse, who wrote *The Natural Garden*, tells me that the city's air pollution acts like a fungicide, so I have that to thank for the fact that from June through October I cut armfuls of roses daily instead of lamenting scourges of black spot, rust, or mildew. The biggest pests our terrace ever encountered were tomato hornworms, and although a few were more than two inches long and were equipped with a thornlike appendage that made them quite frightening, the plants they damaged soon recovered. Once those caterpillars had grown into pretty cream-colored moths, they were carried off by the wind into some other neighborhood to lay their eggs, and our garden was never touched again. Hence I knew nothing of all the insects, not to mention mammals, that can dig up, chew to bits, or trample an earthbound garden in the space of a single night.

My next, and current, garden grows between a stream and our small Victorian house. While we were still negotiating with the previous owners, we visited a friend in Cooperstown, New York, who took us to view her late great-aunt's house. It was unmanageably large, and slated for demolition. That sort of fate for a wonderful old place made us all a little sad, so we wandered in silence around the grounds. But as we came around to the front of the property, I don't think there was one of us who didn't gasp. Stretching out before us were two magnificent borders, flanking a wide grass path for several hundred feet. My friend had seen the borders many times before, but even she was astonished by their beauty — it was one of those rare and wonderful moments in the life of a garden when all the plants seem to be at peak flowering on the same day.

I didn't notice everything that was in flower then, but I remember enormous drifts of dark-blue Aconitum, and blazing patches of intensely perfumed yellow Hemerocallis, threaded with the dainty blue flowers of Adenophora. Both borders also had wonderful stands of burgundy and pale-pink Alcea rosea, and clouds of white Gypsophila billowed throughout.

This was the borders' swan song, for they were to be plowed under with the house. It is a tribute to our friend that when I asked if I could dig up a number of plants and take them to a new home she agreed, and that when I pressed my luck and asked if she could stall the bulldozers until after a frost or two, she wasn't as horrified as she ought to have been. It was late July, and by our friend's calculations, we had until early October, at best, to buy our house and prepare our garden.

Before the ink had dried on the check that purchased our new house, a backhoe was lumbering up the driveway to dig two trenches, each about a hundred feet long and ten feet wide, on the only piece of clear and somewhat level ground we had. That was mid-September, which gave us only a few weekends to shake precious topsoil out of the heavy clumps of turf the backhoe had peeled back, plus countless bales of peat moss, into the future borders.

Finally, one crisp Friday in early October, I climbed into the biggest station wagon that Hertz could provide and headed off to Cooperstown. I dug all day Saturday, and most of Sunday, dragging clumps of plant roots the size of big tires into the back of the station wagon. When I got into the car on Monday morning to head the four hours south, there were spiders dangling from the rearview mirror and slugs clambering around on the windows and across the seats.

Anyone who has ever worried about what a bunch of healthy perennials can withstand should know that the majority of those plants spent about a month piled on top of each other in our barn. It was quite cold, which helped, and each weekend I soaked them with the hose. By the time the last one was in, the top three inches of the ground was frozen hard; I had to break through the crust to set in the plants, and then cover them thickly with leaves. The plants not only survived but put on a performance the following summer that had total strangers coming up the driveway to gawk.

The magnificence of the borders that first summer had everything to do with the plants' health and, more important, with the fact that the colors, heights, and textures had been chosen by my friend's great-aunt. I have since discovered that her borders were famous in horticultural circles. Mine are only a distillation of hers, but still, I had been handed a can't-fail garden. My carload of plants were compatible both in their cultural requirements and in their combined visual effect — all I had to do was water them and wait.

However haphazard and experimental my own gardens have been, I have loved them all. But I realized that even though I had approached border-making three times, I still had no idea how to do it. The successes I'd had could all be chalked up to luck — I knew nothing of method or technique. So I decided to write the book that would have helped me out. The gardeners interviewed were immensely gracious with their knowledge; I hope you will find the information they shared with me helpful. By way of encouragement, I'd like to offer a bit of wisdom that I've gleaned from my travels. Making a border is a lot like choreographing a group of two-year-olds. You will get a dance, and though it may not precisely be what you expected, it will always be delightful.

Introduction

In the short century since border making's great popularity started, "border" has become a confusing term on both sides of the Atlantic. The technical definition is a narrow planting along some division or boundary in a garden, be it walkway, wall, road, or lawn. What falls under the definition can include a mixture of plants or only a single species, from the most permanent of shrubs to the most tender annual, but to be absolutely correct, the term can't refer to plantings that are unrelated to a garden's margins. These are properly called "beds."

In common garden parlance, however, the line between a bed and a border is vague. The definition has been further muddied by the fact that the high art of the mixed border has become popular, so "border" now implies a fabulous tapestry of different plants, regardless of its placement, and "bed" is applied to smaller and simpler plantings. Since this book is about designing borders, and not about the broader art of landscape design, and since a "bed" placed in the middle of a lawn poses many of the same design questions as does a true border, I have gone with the popular definition.

The turn-of-the-century English garden designer Gertrude Jekyll, whose work continues to be influential, is broadly credited with the invention of the classic herbaceous perennial border; in fact, she popularized a trend that had been started when she was a girl. At the time of her birth, in 1843, herbaceous perennials were unfashionable; considered too rough and simple to warrant attention, they were grown in rows like peas and brussels sprouts and cut for arrangements in the house. (The more predominant form of gardening was called carpetbedding—using low, spreading annuals planted in patterns reminiscent of exotic Persian rugs.)

When Miss Jekyll was still a child, the Victorians romanticized the idea of the "cottage garden," and it soon became a favorite vernacular for planting. Real cottage gardens were imagined to have been filled with hardy plants, and a mythology evolved about the loss of perennials and their rediscovery in the yards of poor cottages. Of course, perennials were being cultivated all along in thousands of gardens untouched by every whim of fashion, but the link with something old and humble made perennials that much more romantic.

By the time Miss Jekyll began writing her many books and articles on gardening, perennials had entered not just the fashionable garden but the formal garden, and they were being planted in huge, mixed borders along walls and walkways. The controversy of the time was whether to dot plants of different colors throughout a border, to avoid sharp color transitions, or to plant in larger clumps. Miss Jekyll was opposed to "the old haphazard sprinkle of colouring" (*Wood and Garden*, Longmans Green & Co., 1899, p. 109) for all but the smallest borders, and advocated planting in long, narrow drifts. This way, she explained, when one group finished flowering, it didn't leave a noticeable hole, for the groups in front and behind could quickly fill in. Her own two-hundred-foot border at Munstead Wood in Surrey was a showcase for her theories and exemplified some of the finest gardening of the day.

When Miss Jekyll died in 1932, her border had become synonymous with unexcelled design. Her suggestions had taken on the weight of gospel, not just in England but in this country, too, where many gardeners, particularly beginning gardeners, had an inferiority complex with respect to their English counterparts.

Even today we tend to think that the English climate is more hospitable, their soil better, their pestilences less damaging, and their architecture more befitting great horticultural endeavors than anything we have here.

In fact, many an English gardener would do anything to have the long, hot summers that much of our country enjoys. Familiar annuals, such as petunias, zinnias, tagetes (marigolds), and salvias, tolerate the misty English climate, but it is here that they are at their best. Americans can grow most of the world's tropical perennials as annuals, something the cooler, moister English summer doesn't generally permit.

The same misty blue light that makes English gardens so romantic turns colors such as red cold and hard, yet in the warm yellow light of our summers, the reds, oranges, and golds are wonderfully hot and dazzling. Our scenery is different, too. We may not have England's enviable rolling pastureland and ancient, mellow stonework, but we have extraordinary natural vistas of mountains and oceans. So whereas hedges or walls enclose the prototypical English garden, American gardeners often use their gardens to set off a breathtaking view.

The differences in climate, topography, and setting have given rise to differences in design, and nowhere is this more evident than in our borders. Lacking England's tradition of enormous gardens, our perspective, especially for private gardens, is smaller-scaled. Turn-of-the-century English gardeners could create different areas within a garden for different parts of the summer. In this country, the garden writer Louise Beebe Wilder suggested in her 1918 book *Color in My Garden* that a single border have a series of pictures throughout a six-month season, each restricted to a small area or areas, while the rest of the garden remained lush and green with foliage plants. Ms. Wilder's concept that a small garden could deliver as much beauty, for just as much time, as a large one was novel and her outlook has prevailed ever since.

A border is part horticulture, part art, and a good border is a masterpiece of both. It requires accurate knowledge of flowering times, growing requirements, and how to urge plants into performing a bit better, or more often, than nature programmed them to. It means orchestrating color harmonies and balancing forms, while understanding that when you're working with nature, nothing is guaranteed.

Nobody would decorate by assembling favorite furnishings, fabrics, and paint colors and then trying to fit them all into a room; yet many people go right out and buy a carload of their favorite plants and then try to form them into a cohesive border. Chances are the border will bloom nicely, say, in June, and then turn into a mass of yellowing stalks and uninteresting foliage—the interior designer's equivalent of ordering all the beautiful chintz-covered sofas and chairs but forgetting necessities such as lamps and end tables.

The solution lies not just in planning ahead but in knowing how—which is a matter of knowing how to select what you need. Experienced gardeners see plants from several perspectives. One tells them about a plant's value in a border over the entire summer, only a very tiny aspect of which is the plant's bloom time. Hostas, for example, have lovely foliage from June through frost, and their late-summer flowers are pretty but considered by many to be incidental. A Hosta, therefore, will never leave an ugly brown hole in a border. Oriental poppies, however, bloom in early June, only to brown off immediately after. Most gardeners don't value poppies less, but they recognize the trade-off for all that glorious bloom. They must either live with brown leaves, plant some annuals amid them, or plant something next to them that will broaden and cover their dying foliage, such as Limonium.

A second aspect to a plant is its form. Some plants, such as Aruncus dioicus (goatsbeard), are soft and blowsy; others, such as Onopordum, are boldly geometric. Most garden designers would advise offsetting masses of the former with a specimen or two of the latter. Height enters into the question of form, too: Artemisia ludoviciana is a low to mid-height plant with a soft lacy shape, whereas Hostas are in the same height range but are crisper and more sculptural.

The most obvious thing about a plant is the color

of its flowers. But while most of us see a Delphinium as a beautiful blue, an experienced gardener will note whether it is a lavender-blue (a pinkish blue tinted with white), true deep sky-colored blue, or a violet (reddish) tone. Seeing the differences, a gardener knows that a pale-yellow flower will blend softly with the first, less softly with the second, and contrast vividly with the third.

Given this cross-reference system of form, foliage, and color, it becomes easier to wade through a plant catalog and put together a simple border. Begin with some plants with attractive foliage that holds all summer (small shrubs and grasses are worth considering here) to tide the border over when things aren't flowering. If you choose, accent a border that tends to be too fluffy with something sculptural. Verbascum and Onopordum are wonderful for this, but are biennials that need to be cut down when they start to fade in midsummer; for permanence some people opt for one of the columnar evergreens. At this stage you have a framework that will hold a border together throughout the summer. What remains is to choose your color scheme, and to decide if you want to concentrate bloom times around one or two specific periods or try to stretch your border into a full-season event.

From the beginning, I have based this book on the assumption that gardeners, like cooks, can learn by imitating their peers. If anyone can try a new recipe by following the instructions set out in a cookbook, then, given the guidelines, anyone ought to be able to reproduce a pretty border. The plans for the seventeen gardens shown here are tried and true. Like most recipes, these will work wonderfully if you follow them to the letter, and they can also suffer a little educated meddling without ill effect. The idea is to inspire, as well as to inform. When in doubt about substituting one plant for another, check with the people in your neighborhood who know best: local nurseries, other gardeners, the nearest arboretum. Garden people are nothing if not generous with their knowledge.

CHAPTER ONE

Small Package

Mary Philbrick is a perfect role model for anyone who finds that garden design can be overly abstract. Though familiar with all the theories — as a librarian, she has ample opportunity to study gardening history — she refuses to get bogged down in them. Her little stocking-shaped border pulls together an unconventional mix of the ordinary, the stylish, and the marginally out-of-date, and transforms it into a paradise of flowers.

Mrs. Philbrick explains that she crams her border with flowers (rather than foliage plants) because it is set on a sweeping backdrop of deep green — even the horizon is filled with the blowsy forms of the huge shade trees that surround her lawn. The blooming times of the plants she has selected provide continuous color to ensure that the border stands out against its verdant backdrop.

As a result, she grows a huge variety of plants for so small a border. "I know my border looks as if I throw everything in but the kitchen sink," says Mrs. Philbrick, "but it seems to look pretty through most of the summer and early fall." The trade-off for having lots of different colors in a small space, and a reasonably long flowering season, is that there is room for only a small clump of each variety.

When Mary Philbrick and her husband came to this house in November 1959, the stocking-shaped border was already there, planted with only violets and some bulbs. It adjoined a bed filled with flowering quince (Chaenomeles) bushes, "a terrible pain in the neck," Mrs. Philbrick says, because, although the blossoms are lovely, the bushes are thorny and scraggly, and easily spread into a thicket.

The quince came out, as did the violets, and Mary Philbrick began to fill the little border with a mixture of flowers. Though right on Narragansett Bay, where you might expect to find sandy soil, the garden has heavy clay soil, and

Tiny but color-packed, Mary Philbrick's stocking-shaped border is the more dazzling for its plain green backdrop.

ABOVE: *The border peaks in mid-July, sporting small clumps of every conceivable color.*

LEFT: *At the "heel" and "ankle" are Geum quellyon, Centaurea montana, Veronica 'Blue Peter', and Gypsophila paniculata.*

RIGHT: *In the "toe," Monarda Cambridge Scarlet and Chrysanthe-*

mum x superbum Alaska crowd a red-and-yellow Hemerocallis.

because it sits in a little hollow, drainage is a problem. Although Mrs. Philbrick added a lot of sand and peat moss to improve conditions, certain plants still sulk or outright refuse to grow. One is Delphinium, which she has learned to treat as an annual. "That isn't really such a bad thing with a garden this small," she says, "because I need only six or seven."

The stocking border starts off in spring with late tulips. It progresses with columbine and peonies, for, as Mrs. Philbrick says, "who could have a garden without peonies?" But the border's real season is July, when Mrs. Philbrick's beloved Veronica, feverfew (Chrysanthemum parthenium), and miniature roses are at their best. This, too, is when the Delphinium, Phlox, Monarda, and Achillea are in bloom, all of them eye-popping bright. The border doesn't fade quietly into late summer, but charges right into early November with the brightness of white Boltonia, pink and blue Aster, and annuals such as Cleome in white and strong pink, bright blue Salvia, and red Pelargonium.

In all her choices, Mary Philbrick displays an astute sense of what will work in her garden, and a cheerful disregard for fashion. She is aware of the popularity of pastel colors, foliage plants, and perennials, but she grows a zestfully colored mix of flowers that leans heavily on annuals. "I know I'm not getting those Gertrude-like drifts of impressionistic, soft color," she says, but points out that she sprinkles her plants around in tiny groups, because her border is far too small for the generous sweeps of color that Gertrude Jekyll urged. And while she could have backed her border with a hedge or a wall to keep the viewer's eye from wandering off into the distance, perhaps she sensed that her huge trees were foil enough and that her green horizon was sufficient containment; her little gem of a border can hold its own. She refuses to have grasses, Red Salvia, Gladiolus, Red-hot Pokers (Kniphofia), and all manner of Dahlias.

The middle of the border is a mass of Achillea 'Coronation Gold', Heliopsis, Gypsophila, pink Phlox paniculata, and Delphinium elatum.

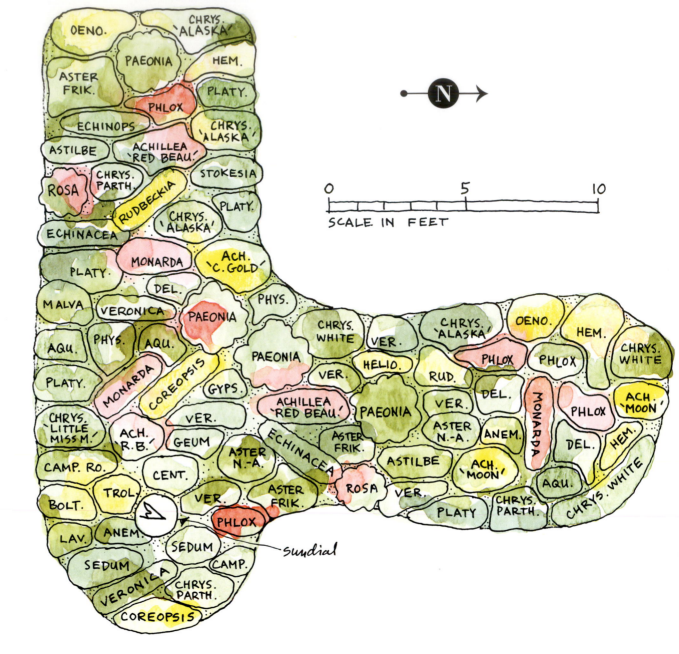

*Garden of
Mary Philbrick
Barrington,
Rhode Island*

SITE: Sun

SOIL: Neutral,
      sandy loam

ZONE: 7a

PLANT LIST

PERENNIALS

Achillea 'Coronation Gold',
'Moonshine', and 'Red Beauty'
Yarrow

Anemone x hybrida 'Alba' and
pink *Japanese anemone*

Aquilegia x hybrida, blue, pink,
and yellow *Columbine*

Aster x frikartii

A. novae-angliae cvs.
New England aster

Astilbe x arendsii 'Deutschland'

Boltonia asteroides 'Snowbank'

Campanula rotundifolia *Bluebell,
Common harebell*

Centaurea montana
Mountain bluet

Chrysanthemum, late-blooming
white

C. parthenium (Matricaria)
Feverfew

C. x superbum 'Alaska' and
'Little Miss Muffet'
Shasta daisy

Coreopsis 'Goldfink' *Tickseed*

Delphinium elatum hybrids

Echinacea purpurea, red
Coneflower

Echinops ritro *Small globe thistle*

Geum quellyon, orange

Gypsophila paniculata 'Bristol
Fairy' *Baby's-breath*

Heliopsis, single yellow
False sunflower

Hemerocallis, yellow and red/
yellow hybrids *Daylily*

Lavandula 'Hidcote'

Malva moschata 'Alba'
Musk mallow

Monarda didyma 'Cambridge
Scarlet' and 'Croftway Pink'
Bee balm, Oswego tea

Oenothera missourensis
Evening primrose

Paeonia, red and pink hybrids
Peony

Phlox paniculata 'Bright Eyes',
'White Admiral', and pale
pink *Garden phlox*

Physostegia virginiana 'Summer
Snow' *Obedient plant*

Platycodon grandiflorus
Balloon flower

Rosa, miniature red and salmon

Rudbeckia fulgida 'Goldsturm'
Black-eyed Susan

Sedum telephium 'Autumn Joy'
Stonecrop

Stokesia laevis, blue *Stokes' aster*

Trollius, yellow *Globeflower*

Veronica spicata 'Blue Peter',
'Icicle', and 'Red Fox'
Speedwell

ANNUALS

Calendula, yellow, in clumps
along edges

Cleome, pink and white, toward
middle of sock, and
mid-"foot" and "leg"

Pelargonium, pink and red,
along edges

Salvia, tall blue, in clumps
throughout

Tagetes, dwarf yellow, in clumps
along edges *Marigold*

Zinnia, dwarf pink, in clumps
along edges

*At the top of the "sock,"
Chrysanthemum x
superbum 'Alaska' spills
over the lawn, flanked by
annual Salvia, Platycodon
grandiflorus, Rudbeckia
fulgida 'Goldsturm', and
Phlox paniculata.*

A Professional's Favorites

When the time comes to design a border, a gardener can elect one of two methods. The first, and safer one, is to begin with when you want it to bloom, proceed to choosing colors, and then, at the very end, decide which plants will satisfy these aims. The other, very unprofessional route is to buy up all your favorite plants and then try to make a border out of them.

Despite her years as a professional garden designer, Cynthia Clark employed the second method for her own border, which started as a way to bring her favorite blooms from the cutting fields closer to her house. She wasn't willing to forfeit any of them for the sake of a more regimented border, so she decided she would find a way to make them all work together. At eighteen by thirty feet, the Clark border is on the small side, but it contains every color from bright red and orange to magenta, lime green, and lavender. Amazingly, none of the colors clash — the effect of the border is soft, even peaceful.

Ms. Clark pulls this off by surrounding loud colors with calmer, but related, tones. So Lychnis coronaria, which is as strong a magenta as you can get, flowers five feet away from a stand of acid-yellow Thermopsis caroliniana. Between the two, however, are the soft lavender-blue of Salvia pratensis and the rose-pink sprays of Lythrum virgatum 'Morden Gleam'. The fact that there is only a little bit of Lychnis helps, too — it is a glint, not a glare.

These all bloom in early June, at a time when you'll find the bright-red climbing rose 'Blaze' along with both white Achillea millefolium and A. 'Coronation Gold', whose dense, flat flowers hover above the foliage like so many chrome-yellow flying saucers. But the red and white are bridged by the pink of Phlox carolina 'Rosalinde' and Digitalis purpurea; the red and yellow by orange Hemerocallis. All of this happens

Cynthia Clark's border spreads like an apron from her front porch, and marks the boundary between lawn and wood.

within close quarters, creating a tightly constructed chiaroscuro. Earlier in the season, Ms. Clark manages the potentially strident meeting of chartreuse Alchemilla mollis and red Papaver orientale by keeping some pink (Centaurea dealbata 'Rose'), lavender-blue (Salvia pratensis), and pale blue (Polemonium caeruleum) between them.

The job of making all these colors get along would have been simpler if the border had been long and narrow, giving Ms. Clark the option of simply isolating color groups. But her border is broad and block-shaped. Furthermore, people see it from all sides with equal frequency (as well as from the porch and from the little path down the middle), so Ms. Clark had no real "front" or "back" to design around. From one angle or another, each flower would be seen with every neighbor.

Year to year, too, the garden changes, partly from attrition (in a particularly cold winter, or dry summer, foxglove seedlings will fail, producing a foxgloveless summer a year later), and partly because of the constant flow of both ideas and plant life in and out of Ms. Clark's gardens. When she found that the native white yarrow (Achillea millefolium) wilted when it was cut, she pulled it out of her cutting fields and replaced it with a cultivated variety ("cultivar") of the same species. She liked the new plant so much that she moved some clumps into the border. The daylilies in the border were castoffs from a client, and the Lychnis coronaria arrived as seed, probably in the roots of the daylilies.

When Matricaria (Chrysanthemum parthenium) started poking up throughout her garden, Ms. Clark discovered that it was due to seeds, and the fact that the plant roots from cuttings with alarming ease. In her spring cleanup, any little fragment of Matricaria that found its way to the ground was as likely to take root as not. She now takes cuttings as soon as the plants begin to grow (on Cape Cod, in March) and pops them into a rooting solution, and by June she has huge plants, ready to be sold to her nursery customers.

Lavender also grows beautifully in this garden, benefitted by Cape Cod's light, sandy soil and relatively mild winters. Ms. Clark limes it to compensate for acid soil (a heavy hand with the lime also produces pinkish flowers), fertilizes fall and spring with cotton-seed meal, and harvests armloads in the summer.

Of all the plants that prosper in her garden, Alchemilla mollis is Cynthia Clark's favorite. Receiving no special treatment, it rewards her by growing into a wide fringe at the lower end of the border. It starts off in late May with blue-green leaves and chartreuse flowers that continue through the second week in July, at which point Ms. Clark cuts it back to bring on a second flush of leaves. Beloved because of the way its felted, scallop-shaped leaves hold on to beads of water after a shower, this plant is a treasure. But I had never fully appreciated how it got its common name, lady's-mantle, until I saw it growing here like a blue-green satin cloak, edged in a froth of paler green lace.

OPPOSITE: *Every border has a plant that favors its owner by seeming to be particularly happy in its home—here it is Alchemilla mollis, which fringes the entire lower end of the border. Behind it are* Chrysanthemum parthenium *and* Digitalis purpurea. RIGHT: *Simple, common plants are used to great advantage in the Clark border.* Rudbeckia fulgida *'Goldsturm', though weedlike in its propensity to spread, is a mainstay of the late-summer show.*

*Garden of
Cynthia Clark
Harwich,
Massachusetts*

SITE: Full sun

SOIL: Sandy, acid

ZONE: 7a

PLANT LIST

PERENNIALS
Achillea 'Coronation Gold' and
   'Moonshine' *Yarrow*
A. millefolium white cv.
   Lady's-mantle
Alchemilla mollis
   Lady's-mantle
Artemisia ludoviciana 'Silver
   King'
Campanula carpatica 'Blue Clips'
   Tussock bellflower
Centaurea dealbata 'Rose'
Chrysanthemum parthenium
   (Matricaria) *Feverfew*
C. x superbum *Shasta daisy*
Coreopsis verticillata
   'Moonbeam' *Tickseed*
Dianthus, pink
Digitalis grandiflora
   (D. ambigua) *Yellow foxglove*
D. purpurea *Common foxglove*
Echinacea purpurea
   Coneflower
Gypsophila paniculata 'Bristol
   Fairy' *Baby's-breath*
Hemerocallis, orange and yellow
   Daylily
Hosta, variegated
Iris x germanica, purple
   Bearded iris
I. sibirica, blue *Siberian iris*
Lavandula angustifolia
   subsp. angustifolia
   (L. vera) *Lavender*
L. 'Munstead'
Lobelia x gerardii, purple
Lychnis coronaria *Rose campion*
Lythrum virgatum 'Morden
   Gleam' *Loosestrife*
Miscanthus sinensis 'Morning
   Light'
Nepeta *Catmint*
Papaver orientale, salmon and
   red *Oriental poppy*
Phlox paniculata, blue and white
   Garden phlox
P. carolina 'Rosalinde'
Physostegia virginiana 'Pink
   Bouquet' *Obedient plant*

Polemonium caeruleum
   Jacob's-ladder
Potentilla fruticosa, yellow
   Cinquefoil
Rudbeckia fulgida 'Goldsturm'
   Black-eyed Susan
Salvia pratensis (S. haematodes)
   Meadow clary
Sedum purpureum 'Autumn Joy'
   Stonecrop
Stokesia laevis 'Blue Danube'
   Stokes' aster
Thermopsis caroliniana
   Carolina lupine

ANNUALS (*self-sown, and random placements*)
Centaurea cyanus
   Bachelor's-button
Coreopsis lanceolata, self-seeded
   throughout border *Tickseed*
Ferns
Lilium hybrids, scattered
   throughout

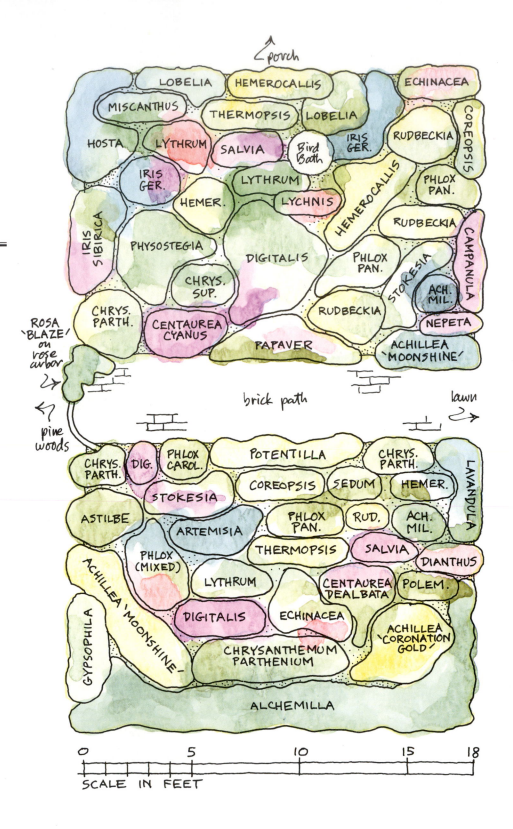

Mixed with a deft hand are the unlikely combination of magenta Lychnis coronaria, deep rose-pink Lythrum virgatum 'Morden Gleam', and lavender Salvia pratensis. Scattered throughout are patches of self-seeded Coreopsis lanceolata.

The Discreet Gardener

The word *border* brings to mind a certain geometry; we expect, at the very least, straight edges and right angles as an indication that man had a hand in its creation. Most gardeners agree that this is a pleasing contrast to the loose, informal nature of plants. You will thus see many a perennial spilling out over a border's straight, crisp edge of turf, and many a luxuriant vine flowing up over the top of a solid brick wall.

Mrs. Morgan Parker's borders are the antithesis of all that. There is not a hard, straight line in her garden. The borders have wavy edges, and plants tumble over them onto the lawn. A fence, not of sawn and painted lumber but of rustic timber with branches and peeling bark, discreetly encloses one end of the garden. Behind the main, western border a mixture of tall, vase-shaped Syringa, big, spreading Philadelphus, and smaller, round Spiraea has grown into a backdrop that resembles not so much a hedge as a thicket. Even within the borders you won't find a bold,

chiseled plant. Everything here is soft and lush.

Visitors to this garden are always overcome by it, for the simple reason that it looks completely natural. Two borders sweep around an expanse of lawn, giving the feeling that where the mower stops, the flowers spring forth on their own. But for all its apparent artlessness, this is probably the hardest kind of garden to design.

Mrs. Parker had no intention of designing anything when she moved to this farm with her husband in 1928. They named it Bylane, which it is, and started gardening. The borders follow the contours of the land and are filled, simply, with plants that she wished to grow. She wanted the borders to look as though nature had put them there, in a meadow partly shaded by huge maples and outlined by lichen-covered stone walls,

---

Flanked by a rustic fence, a stone toolshed, and an ancient lilac, Mrs. Parker's border is filled with old-fashioned flowers such as single Alceas, Phlox, Stachys, Achillea, and Hemerocallis.

and added nothing that would alter that impression. Not once has she broken rank and put in, say, a piece of statuary, or punctuated the border with an accent plant. The garden is a model of consistency.

Colorwise, Mrs. Parker displays the sensitive eye of the artist. The garden peaks in July, and for the July show in the western border, she uses a range of bluish-pinks and violets, and a group of chromium, or greenish, yellows. These two groups lie opposite each other on the color spectrum, which is a good indication that they will work well together in a garden. (Yellowish pinks, or salmons, on the other hand, would have fought mightily with the blue-pink range, and whereas clashes such as this can be successful, they lead to a completely different feeling in a garden. The same can be said of the combination of reddish yellows with greenish yellows.)

Mrs. Parker wrests from her two-color scheme a border of startling complexity. Using dark and light tones of the same color, she makes it look as though dappled sunlight floods her garden. Posing as areas of shade are the darker violet-pinks of Monarda, and the burgundy of some of the hollyhocks. Paler pink hollyhocks and phlox affect patches of sunlight. A small clump of white Lilium candidum, patches of silvery Stachys byzantina, and the bright yellows of the Hemerocallis and Achillea fairly glare with the intensity of an imagined sun. And, of course, the dark- and light-green foliage of the variegated Hosta mimics dappled light all on its own.

Mrs. Parker maintains that the best time to see her garden is at dusk. As the sun lowers itself behind the western border, the effect is indeed magical. In the slanting light, the wavy outline of the border seems to fall along the shadow line cast by the shrubs that grow at the back of the border. Where the shrubs are a little taller, the border is a little broader, and where the shrubs are smaller, the border in front of them becomes narrower. In that light more than in any other, it is easy to imagine that nature really did put the borders here.

In mid-July, a large clump of Echinops ritro anchors the north end of the border. Around it are Achillea 'Coronation Gold', single Alcea rosea, and fragrant Hemerocallis Hyperion. OPPOSITE: *Soft, apparently random plantings are the key to the success of this wavy-edged border.*

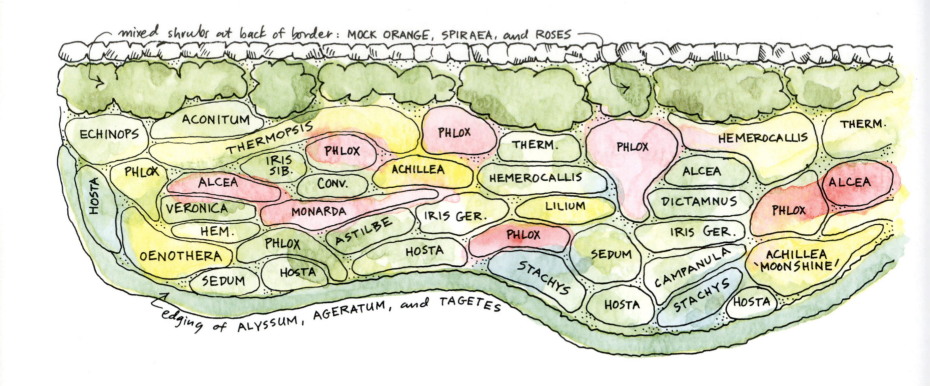

mixed shrubs at back of border: MOCK ORANGE, SPIRAEA, and ROSES

ACONITUM
ECHINOPS
THERMOPSIS
PHLOX
PHLOX
THERM.
HEMEROCALLIS
THERM.
PHLOX
IRIS SIB.
PHLOX
HOSTA
PHLOX
ALCEA
CONV.
ACHILLEA
HEMEROCALLIS
ALCEA
ALCEA
VERONICA
MONARDA
DICTAMNUS
PHLOX
HEM.
ASTILBE
IRIS GER.
LILIUM
IRIS GER.
OENOTHERA
PHLOX
HOSTA
PHLOX
SEDUM
ACHILLEA 'MOONSHINE'
SEDUM
HOSTA
STACHYS
CAMPANULA
HOSTA
HOSTA
STACHYS
HOSTA

edging of ALYSSUM, AGERATUM, and TAGETES

"Bylane"
Garden of
Mrs. Morgan Parker
Westchester County,
New York

SITE: Full sun

SOIL: Slightly acid, well-drained
  loam

ZONE: 6a

PLANT LIST

PERENNIALS
Achillea 'Coronation Gold'
  Yarrow
Aconitum napellus *Monkshood*
Alcea rosea, singles *Hollyhock*
Anthemis tinctoria
  Golden marguerite
Astilbe chinensis 'Pumila'
Brunnera macrophylla
  Siberian bugloss

Campanula persicifolia
  Willow bellflower
Clematis paniculata
  Sweet autumn clematis
Convallaria majalis
  Lily-of-the-valley
Dictamnus albus *Gas-plant*
Echinops ritro *Small globe thistle*
Gypsophila paniculata
  Baby's-breath
Heliopsis helianthoides
  False sunflower
Hemerocallis 'Hyperion' *Daylily*
Hosta lancifolia, solid green and
  variegated
Iberis sempervirens *Candytuft*
Iris x germanica *Bearded iris*
I. sibirica *Siberian iris*
Lavatera *Tree mallow*
Lilium candidum *Madonna lily*
Monarda didyma 'Violet Queen'
  Bee balm, Oswego tea
Nemesia
Oenothera tetragona (O. fruticosa

var. youngii) *Evening primrose*
Phlox paniculata *Garden phlox*
Polemonium caeruleum
  Jacob's-ladder
Sedum purpureum 'Autumn Joy'
  Stonecrop
Stachys byzantina (S. lanata)
  Lamb's-ear
Thermopsis caroliniana
  Carolina lupine
Veronica spicata *Speedwell*

ANNUALS
Ageratum
Alyssum
Nierembergia hippomanica
Tagetes *Marigold*

SHRUBS AND VINES
Buxus *Box*

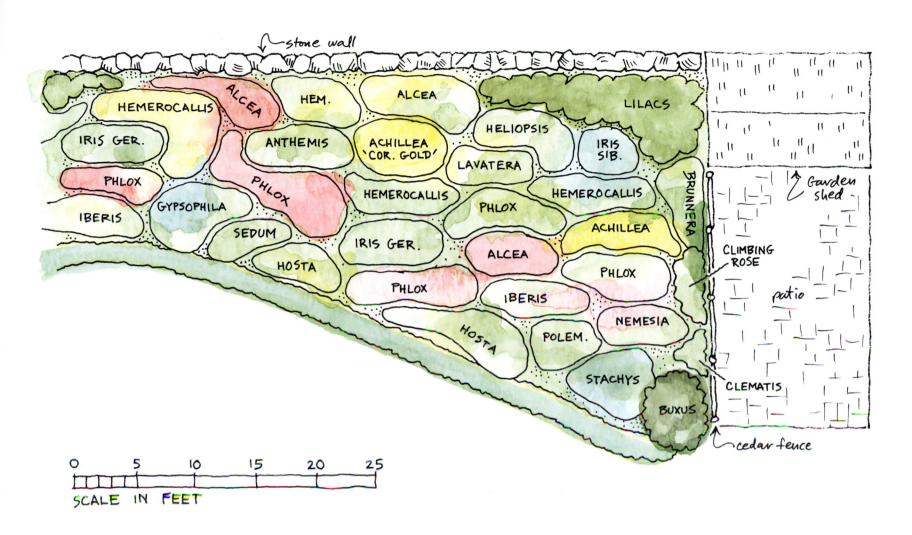

stone wall

HEMEROCALLIS
ALCEA
HEM.
ALCEA
LILACS
IRIS GER.
ANTHEMIS
ACHILLEA 'COR. GOLD'
HELIOPSIS
IRIS SIB.
PHLOX
PHLOX
LAVATERA
GYPSOPHILA
HEMEROCALLIS
HEMEROCALLIS
IBERIS
SEDUM
PHLOX
ACHILLEA
HOSTA
IRIS GER.
ALCEA
PHLOX
PHLOX
IBERIS
NEMESIA
HOSTA
POLEM.
STACHYS
BUXUS

BRUNNERA

Garden shed

CLIMBING ROSE

patio

CLEMATIS

cedar fence

0	5	10	15	20	25

SCALE IN FEET

In late June, Oenothera tetragona, with the apt common name of sun-drops, brightens large areas of the border.

Shrubs as a Mainstay

Ann Howell grew up in Malaysia, so her childhood memories are filled with the spicy colors of lush tropical gardens (through the gates of which Santa Claus used to arrive aboard his elephant). Later her family moved to England, where colors are softer and paler. So when Mrs. Howell came to this country and began her own garden, her visual aesthetic was linked to both extremes. Throughout her main border in New York's Westchester County runs a line of shrubs such as Weigela, Clethra, and Deutzia, a feature that reflects the traditional English mixed border. But in front of the shrubs, she has chosen and positioned plants to create color pyrotechnics.

The Howell border has many mandates. It must be pretty from the verandah, which, because the house is on a steep slope, is some twenty feet above the border. It must look good from the lawn that it edges, because people walk and eat lunch there. And it must be interesting all year long, for it is in constant view. Getting all of this out of any border would be hard — but for a border that is a hundred feet long and barely eight feet deep, it takes very careful planning.

Much of this work is done by the shrubs. Thirteen different varieties were chosen for their year-round form and color, and are planted all through the border, not just at the back. Bloom begins in early April with the froth of bright-yellow flowers that covers the bare branches of Cornus mas. In May come the Viburnum carlesii's fragrant white clusters, followed in late May by Prunus x cistena and Deutzia. June brings the rose-pink flowers of Weigela and the white blossoms of Cornus kousa, which gradually become suffused with pink and can last for a month if the weather doesn't get too hot. The pale salmon-pink rose 'Bonica' begins its summer–

Few plants give as spectacular a fall show as the North American natives, the asters. This one, 'Harrington's Pink', along with the autumn foliage of shrubs, extends this border's season well into October.

haze of gentian-blue, and soon some of the other shrubs will start to change into their autumn garb: yellow for the Clethra, deep purple for the Hydrangea, and red for the Cornus kousa (plus the constant dark maroon of the Prunus x cistena). Had it not been for the advice of Colin Streeter, a close friend and noted garden designer, the border's interest might have ended in the fall. But in the back of the border, where it is held up by a retaining wall and where Mrs. Howell had thought to plant Clematis and climbing roses, Streeter advised her to plant a procumbent variety of juniper and Cotoneaster apiculatus. Both have sprawled over the edge of the wall, and the combination of the blue-green juniper and the red berries and dark-green foliage of the Cotoneaster is sensational in the snow.

Once she had organized her shrubs so that they would hold the border together almost all year, Mrs. Howell found placing her perennials a relatively easy task. In an attempt to create the same informal jumble of color found in a nineteenth-century cottage garden, she "dotted plants around and didn't fuss about whether colors clashed." Instead of orchestrating gradual color changes, Mrs. Howell created several abrupt ones, placing hot-pink Dianthus beneath an orangy-yellow iris, and the flame-orange Geum quellyon 'Mrs. Bradshaw' beside a baby-pink peony and a mound of chartreuse Alchemilla mollis.

If England's cottage tradition influenced Mrs. Howell's garden, America gave it its final form. America's climate is much more extreme than England's, being arctic in winter and tropical in summer. And whereas Mrs. Howell admits that it makes gardening here harder, it also means that the American spring, though later, "is like a tropical explosion. There is nothing gradual or subdued about it." To Mrs. Howell, this is a bonus, and if hot summers also mean that most plants stay in flower for a shorter time, and cold winters reduce her options, these are things she can tolerate. She adds, "Either you nurture things that don't relish this sort of treatment, or you take those that will survive and do without those your particular microclimate won't accommodate."

ABOVE: A true test of a border's merit is when it is pretty from above, as this one is. **RIGHT:** *Paeonia 'Festiva Maxima' and Weigela 'Bristol Ruby'.*

long flowering in June, joined, of course, by many of the border's perennials. For a brief time in late June and early July, the perennials are the whole show, but then the Clethra opens its intensely fragrant creamy blossoms, followed by the Hydrangea quercifolia.

Come September, the Caryopteris is covered in a

ABOVE: *In early June, the border is radiant with the flowers of a pale-pink Weigela, bright pink Dianthus, the chartreuse Alchemilla, the lavenders and purples of Nepeta and two varieties of Iris x germanica, and the palest pink Paeonia. Adding to the mix are the felted gray foliage of Stachys byzantina and the purple leaves of Prunus x cistena.*

LEFT: *About a week earlier, the Deutzia is covered with white blossoms; the Alchemilla and Nepeta are just opening.*

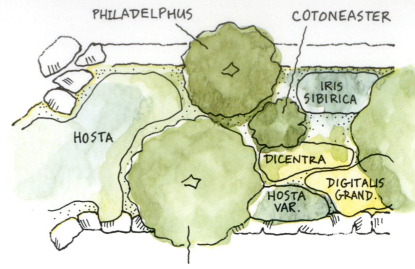

PHILADELPHUS   COTONEASTER

HOSTA

IRIS SIBIRICA

DICENTRA

HOSTA VAR.

DIGITALIS GRAND.

CORNUS KOUSA

Garden of
Ann C. Howell
Westchester County,
New York

SITE: Sunny, with light shade
at each end

SOIL: Slightly acid loam

ZONE: 6b

PLANT LIST

PERENNIALS

Achillea taygetea *Yarrow*
Alchemilla mollis *Lady's-mantle*
Allium Schoenoprasum *Chives*
Anemone x hybrida
Japanese anemone
Artemisia dracunculus
Tarragon
A. ludoviciana 'Silver King'
A. schmidtiana
'Silver Mound'
Aster 'Harrington's Pink'
Astilbe
Caryopteris x clandonensis
Cerastium tomentosum
Snow-in-summer
Coreopsis lanceolata
C. verticillata *Tickseed*
Dianthus, bright pink and white
Dicentra eximia
Wild bleeding-heart
Digitalis grandiflora (D. ambigua)
Yellow foxglove
D. x mertonensis *Foxglove hybrid*
Euphorbia cyparissias
Cypress spurge
Geum quellyon 'Mrs. Bradshaw'
Hemerocallis 'Sun Ruffles' and
yellow *Daylily*
Hosta
H. variegata
Iris x germanica, one with purple
falls and pink-brown
standards; one strong
sun-yellow
Bearded iris
I. sibirica, blue-purple
Siberian iris
Ligularia stenocephala 'The
Rocket'
Lupinus, yellow
Nepeta x faassenii *Catmint*
Paeonia *Peony*
Perovskia atriplicifolia
Russian sage
Phlox carolina 'Miss Lingard'
P. paniculata, pink and white
Garden phlox

Platycodon grandiflorus
Balloon flower
Polygonum *Knotweed*
Salvia officinalis 'Tricolor',
variegated *Garden sage*
Stachys byzantina (S. lanata)
Lamb's-ears

SHRUBS

Clethra alnifolia*
Sweet pepperbush
Cornus kousa*
C. mas* *Cornelian cherry*
Cotoneaster apiculatus**
Deutzia*
Hydrangea quercifolia* *Oak-leaf
hydrangea*
Ilex crenata** *Japanese holly*
Juniperus**
Philadelphus* *Mock orange*
Prunus x cistena*
Purple-leaf sand cherry
Rosa 'Bonica'*
Viburnum carlesii*
Weigela 'Bristol Ruby'*

* deciduous shrubs
**evergreen shrubs

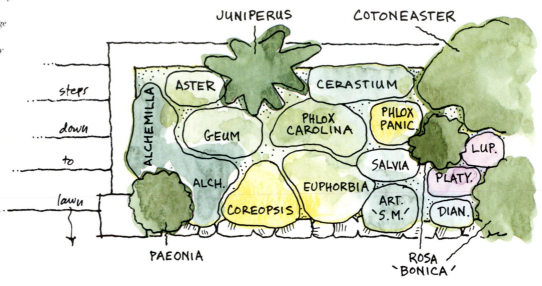

JUNIPERUS   COTONEASTER

steps

down

to

lawn

ALCHEMILLA

ASTER

CERASTIUM

GEUM

PHLOX CAROLINA

PHLOX PANIC.

ALCH.

SALVIA

LUP.

COREOPSIS

EUPHORBIA

ART. 'S.M.'

PLATY.

DIAN.

PAEONIA

ROSA 'BONICA'

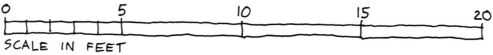

0   5   10   15   20

SCALE IN FEET

N

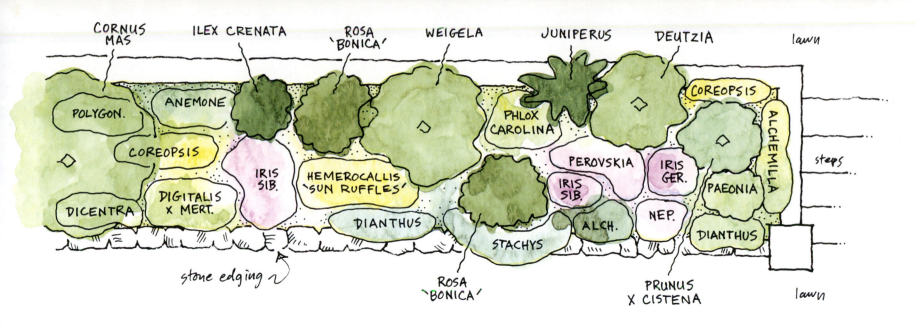

CORNUS MAS · ILEX CRENATA · ROSA 'BONICA' · WEIGELA · JUNIPERUS · DEUTZIA · lawn

POLYGON.

ANEMONE

COREOPSIS

DICENTRA

DIGITALIS x MERT.

IRIS SIB.

HEMEROCALLIS 'SUN RUFFLES'

DIANTHUS

STACHYS

PHLOX CAROLINA

PEROVSKIA

IRIS SIB.

ALCH.

NEP.

IRIS GER.

PAEONIA

DIANTHUS

COREOPSIS

ALCHEMILLA

steps

stone edging

ROSA 'BONICA'

PRUNUS X CISTENA

lawn

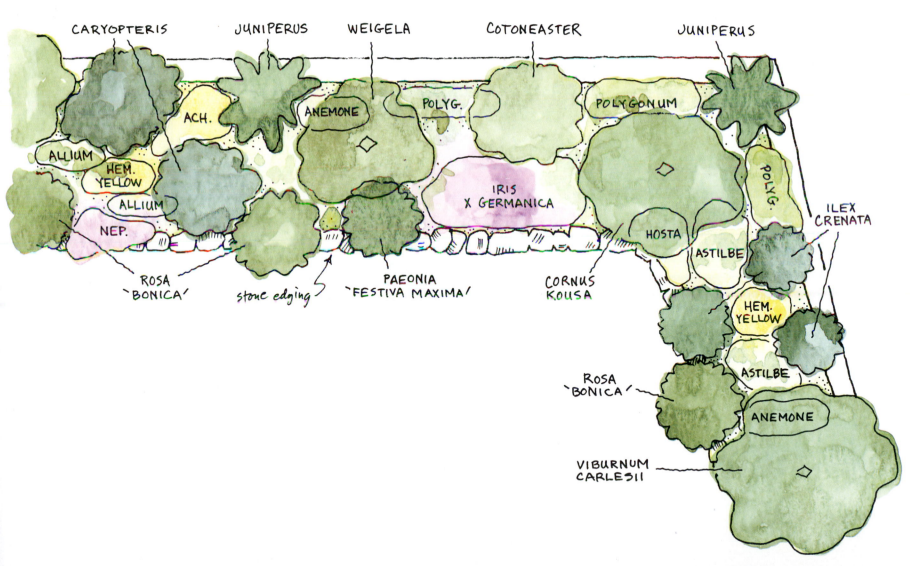

CARYOPTERIS · JUNIPERUS · WEIGELA · COTONEASTER · JUNIPERUS

ALLIUM

HEM. YELLOW

ALLIUM

NEP.

ACH.

ANEMONE

POLYG.

POLYGONUM

IRIS X GERMANICA

HOSTA

ASTILBE

POLYG.

ILEX CRENATA

ROSA 'BONICA'

stone edging

PAEONIA 'FESTIVA MAXIMA'

CORNUS KOUSA

HEM. YELLOW

ASTILBE

ROSA 'BONICA'

ANEMONE

VIBURNUM CARLESII

A Painter's Mountainside Garden

When painter Raymond Han sequesters himself in his studio to transpose the luminous cup-shaped petals of a peony onto canvas, it is by no means the first time he has labored intently over that flower. He planted it, carefully weeded around it, and urged it along all spring, just as he did for more than a hundred of its neighbors. Although Han also paints figures and still lifes, no other subject causes him to work as hard as his flowers do.

When Mr. Han and his companion, Paul Kellogg, bought their property in upstate New York fifteen years ago, it had no garden. Where the main border now grows had once been a barn, though its superstructure was long gone. For generations, all that had remained was a large rectangular pit, and a dirt and gravel ramp that had led up to a hayloft. Previous tenants

Set in the foundation of an old barn, Raymond Han's serene border is a tribute to the artistry and determination of its creator.

had simply driven up the ramp with trucks full of refuse and dumped it over the edge into the old foundation of the barn.

Raymond Han's goal was to get the dump cleared up, sitting as it does about thirty feet from the house, and then plant a border over it. "It seemed so natural to have a garden there," Mr. Han recalls, "but it really wasn't a great idea. Everything spoke against it."

He recounts a saga of enormous rocks lurking just below the earth's surface, which he and Mr. Kellogg had to lever out with a huge iron rod. This, after they had already hauled off tons of tin cans, broken bottles, old bones, and all sorts of other unpleasant detritus. Mr. Han laughs, remembering that he had naively envisioned a foundation filled with magnificent topsoil from decades of accumulated manure. To keep the sheer side of the old ramp from eroding into the border, he and Paul Kellogg faced it with stone, and then they built a low dry wall around the periphery of their new garden. Finally, planting began.

The western part of the border is backed by the shale retaining wall of the old barn, which the owners capped with an ornamental pyramid. At the end of July, the tall creamy plumes of Macleaya, pale-lavender Phlox, Coreopsis, the Astilbe-like Artemisia lactiflora, steel-blue Echinops, and apricot Hemerocallis are in bloom.

The garden is on the side of a mountain, and Mr. Han acknowledges he learned that a mountain remains a mountain because it is made of rock. Less than a foot beneath the surface lies a solid ledge of shale, which means that the soil dries out quickly and plants can't put down very deep roots. The garden is also exposed to everything nature hurls at the sides of mountains, so plants such as hollyhocks (Alcea rosea) and Delphinium, which Mr. Han loves, are out of the question.

Having relived all that labor, which he and Mr. Kellogg did unassisted, Mr. Han added one of the most implausible remarks I'd heard in a long time. "If I were at all serious about gardening, I would have done it in a different way. I would have taken the time to have the beds prepared properly. But I didn't want to go through all that work."

Perhaps he has a point. He could have blasted into the ledge with dynamite, excavated huge trenches for the border, and then laid in drains. Instead, he focused on what would grow in shallow soil on the side of his mountain. He has found Aconitum to be quite content with what he is able to provide, and has added a third variety, A. x bicolor, since we photographed the garden. Phlox paniculata is a mainstay of what he

refers to as the "gaudy" stage of the border, toward the end of July, when it, the daylilies, and most of the other plants are in bloom.

Peonies, Siberian irises, and a profusion of shrub roses dominate the spring show in the garden. Unfortunately, the roses, which thrive locally, were girdled by resident mice, and will take several years to regain their former glory. Mr. Han is philosophical. "In gardening," he says, "the impetus is to somehow rectify calamity." For the roses, he will devise some defense. For other casualties, he says, "I get something from the nearest place and plop it in," suggesting a trip to either a nursery or a friend with superfluous plants.

Raymond Han always wanted a garden that would bloom in late summer and fall. For years, he tried to grow asters, but the plants refused to bloom. "I looked up one day and thought to myself, 'How stupid! Here's this glorious flower, blooming right next to me in a field!'" It was a wild blue aster, which he has now lifted and planted in his border. He also dug up some clumps of the ubiquitous rose-pink flowered Eupatorium purpureum (Joe-Pye weed), which is a late-summer- and fall-blooming native that he imagines will thrive in his border.

Mr. Han's affection for wildflowers is spurred not just because they are obviously attuned to the local climate; he shrinks from many modern cultivars, finding the blooms "so bright, they're really almost fluorescent. And many are *so* large. It's hard to get anything subtle." He relates driving past a garden and being transfixed by a huge stand of pale-pink phlox. "It had tiny flowers, but so many of them, the effect was just beautiful." He stopped his car, knocked on the door of the house, and offered to buy a little clump of the flowers. They now reside in his border, where they have prospered.

Despite the long, frigid winters and brief summers in soil prone to drying, the Han border is hospitable to many more plant varieties than you would expect. The Artemisia that thrives here, for instance, is not one of the silver-leaved species that loves its soil on the dry side but A. lactiflora, the four- to six-foot-tall

species that has beautiful fernlike foliage and creamy panicles of flowers reminiscent of an astilbe. It requires a rich, moist soil. Aconitum loathes having its soil baked dry, as do Iris sibirica, Anemone x hybrida, and Phlox paniculata, yet all grow robustly in Raymond Han's border.

Mr. Han accomplishes this in part because summers in his region see relatively few steaming hot, sultry days. And though not deep, the soil is rich and moisture-retentive. The border is also planted so densely that the sun rarely penetrates down to the soil level. So, although he does water the border from time to time, he doesn't have to coddle it.

Raymond Han doesn't object to hard work, but he expects beauty in return. His pure, lucid paintings always convey the essence of his subjects, something that comes both from diligence and from knowing and admiring what he is painting. Certainly that holds for his floral still lifes, for no one knows how miraculous a flower is better than the person who grew it.

The border here is in what Mr. Han refers to as its "gaudy stage," when the Phlox paniculata, especially the cherry-red variety 'Starfire', fills the border with strong color.

LEFT: *For the border's late July show, a wonderful array of colors jumbles together, including deep purple-blue Aconitum and the steel-blue spheres of Echinops, pink and white Phlox, apricot Hemerocallis, and white Iberis and Chrysanthemum parthenium.*

In the center of the border, a globe-capped obelisk is surrounded by Phlox 'Starfire', the dark-purple Salvia x superba, a white Veronica, and Chrysanthemum parthenium.

*Garden of
Raymond Han
Otsego County,
New York*

Site: Full sun, windy

Soil: Shallow, slightly acid
loam

Zone: 4b

PLANT LIST

PERENNIALS

Aconitum autumnale
  Monkshood
A. fischeri
Ajuga *Bugleweed*
Anemone x hybrida
  Japanese anemone
Artemisia lactiflora
Aster novae-angliae
  'Survivor'
Buddleia davidii *Butterfly bush*
B. fischeri *Butterfly bush*
Chelone obliqua *Turtlehead*
Chrysanthemum parthenium
  (Matricaria) *Feverfew*
C. x superbum *Shasta daisy*
Coreopsis *Tickseed*
Echinops sphaerocephalus
  Great globe thistle
Eupatorium purpureum
  Joe-Pye weed
Geranium sanguineum var.
  prostratum (G. lancastriense)
  Cranesbill
Hemerocallis *Daylily*
Hosta 'Honeybells'
H. ventricosa
Iberis sempervirens *Candytuft*
Iris sibirica 'Caesar's Brother' and
  white *Siberian iris*
Lavandula
Lysimachia clethroides
  Gooseneck loosestrife
Macleaya cordata *Plume poppy*
Oenothera perennis *Sundrops*
Origanum vulgare *Marjoram*
Paeonia 'Festiva Maxima' and
  single white *Peony*

Phlox paniculata 'Bright Eyes',
  'Dodo Hansbury Forbes',
  'Fairy's Petticoat', 'Starfire',
  late pink, late white,
  midseason white, and pale
  lavender *Garden phlox*
Primula japonica *Primrose*
Rosa x alba semiplena
R. centifolia 'York and
  Lancaster'
R. 'Madame Hardy' and pink
  shrub
R. moyesii 'Carnation'
Rosa rugosa
Salvia officinalis *Garden sage*
S. x superba
Sedum purpureum 'Autumn Joy'
  Stonecrop
Thymus vulgaris *Garden thyme*
Veronica

SHRUBS

Philadelphus *Mock orange*
Syringa vulgaris *Lilac*

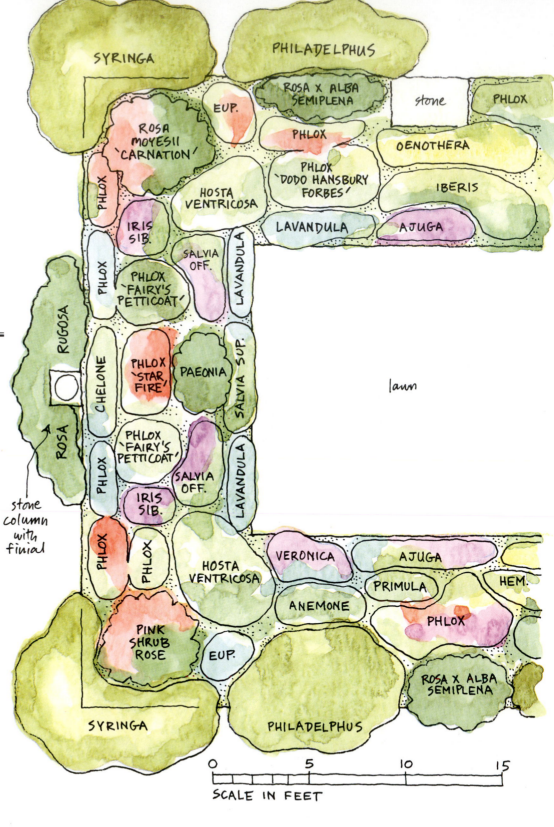

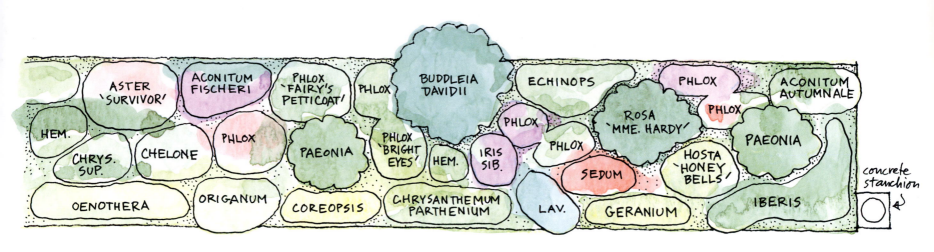

ASTER 'SURVIVOR'
ACONITUM FISCHERI
PHLOX 'FAIRY'S PETTICOAT'
PHLOX
BUDDLEIA DAVIDII
ECHINOPS
PHLOX
ACONITUM AUTUMNALE
HEM.
PHLOX
PHLOX
ROSA 'MME. HARDY'
PHLOX
CHRYS. SUP.
CHELONE
PHLOX
PAEONIA
PHLOX 'BRIGHT EYES'
HEM.
IRIS SIB.
PHLOX
SEDUM
HOSTA 'HONEY BELLS'
PAEONIA
OENOTHERA
ORIGANUM
COREOPSIS
CHRYSANTHEMUM PARTHENIUM
LAV.
GERANIUM
IBERIS
concrete stanchion

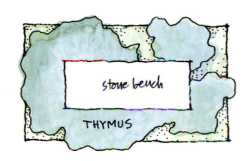

stone bench

THYMUS

lawn

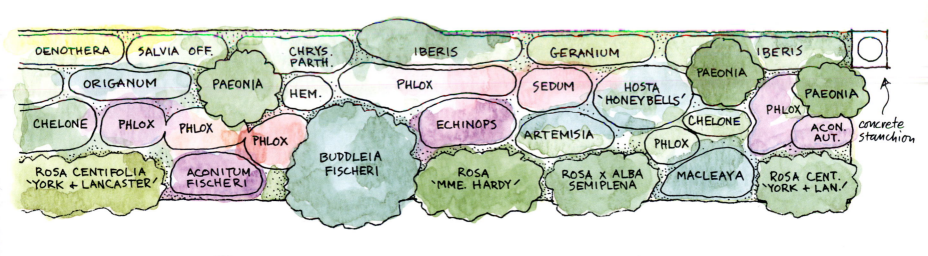

OENOTHERA
SALVIA OFF.
CHRYS. PARTH.
IBERIS
GERANIUM
IBERIS
ORIGANUM
PAEONIA
HEM.
PHLOX
SEDUM
HOSTA 'HONEYBELLS'
PAEONIA
PAEONIA
CHELONE
PHLOX
PHLOX
ECHINOPS
ARTEMISIA
CHELONE
PHLOX
PHLOX
ACON. AUT.
PHLOX
ROSA CENTIFOLIA 'YORK + LANCASTER'
ACONITUM FISCHERI
BUDDLEIA FISCHERI
ROSA 'MME. HARDY'
ROSA X ALBA SEMIPLENA
MACLEAYA
ROSA CENT. 'YORK + LAN.'
concrete stanchion

N

A Gardening Partnership

On any given day of the year, weather permitting, you might find architect Dale Booher and his wife, garden designer Lisa Stamm, sitting on chairs in the middle of their lawn talking. They are not unwinding after a hard day; they are conducting a work session. The topic of discussion will be their own perennial border, which spreads out along the privet hedge in front of them.

In bringing the arts of architecture and garden design together to form a garden, the couple have very distinguished company. Gertrude Jekyll, in her partnership with Sir Edwin Lutyens, established that the relationship between a house and its garden is central to the success of both, and that the whole creation should represent a collaboration between architect and landscape architect. And in 1930, two years before Miss Jekyll died, another famed gardening partnership, Vita Sackville-West and Harold Nicolson, bought the ruin that was Sissinghurst. There they created the garden that is arguably one of the best-known gardens in the world, he serving generally as designer and she as plantswoman.

The Booher-Stamm house, known as The Homestead, benefits from a collaboration that works much the same way as the one that formed Sissinghurst. Mr. Booher creates the bones of the garden, and Ms. Stamm embellishes them with her plants. Just like Ms. Sackville-West and Mr. Nicolson, they bought an improbable site and turned it into something few people would have thought up, let alone thought possible. Once just a tiny saltbox set in the middle of a field, The Homestead has evolved into a charming cottage partly surrounded by tall hedges and screens of espaliered fruit trees. Herbs, vegetables, and cutting flowers grow in allotted spots; other features include a rock garden, a shade garden, a swimming pool amid a rose garden, and several borders.

In the early morning, tall trees dapple the light falling on The Homestead's main border, where the yellow Lilium 'Olivia' and the pale-pink peony 'Sarah Bernhardt' flower behind a clump of Stachys byzantina.

ABOVE: *In mid-July,*
Thalictrum rochebruni-
anum and the annual
Cleome 'Helen Campbell'
stand out against the
privet hedge that runs
along the back of the
border. RIGHT: *Behind*
a clump of Veronica
latifolia 'Crater Lake
Blue' blooms Verbena
bonariensis, grown
here as an annual.

Having designed city gardens for many years, Lisa Stamm knows the importance of plants that hold their form beyond a brief flowering spell. Not only is space at a premium in an urban setting, but such gardens tend to be viewed year-round and close up, which doesn't leave room for plants with short-lived beauty. Consequently, Ms. Stamm's borders show a preponderance of plants such as Thalictrum rochebrunianum (her favorite), Anemone x hybrida, Astilbe, and the Filipendula. All of these form mounds of foliage that look pretty throughout the summer, both from a distance and under closer scrutiny. These plants, combined with the lacy gray-blue foliage of Artemisia 'Powis Castle' and the strappy green leaves of Iris sibirica, I. ensata, and Hemerocallis, create a formula that is uniquely Lisa Stamm's.

Annuals offer gardeners a mesmerizing range of bright colors, and many borders rely on them for midsummer color. Ms. Stamm, who was originally averse to annuals altogether, now uses a few. Still she stayed with the soft tones she prefers, clumping them together in large stands, so that even though the colors aren't powerful, the effect is.

Come September, The Homestead's border puts on a last and spectacular show. All the asters come into flower then, joining the Anemones, Sedums, Helianthus, and some of the annuals. Having been cut down by about half their height in both early June and early July, the asters fountain with flowers, and hold them well into October. In the first week of December, though, the only plant still holding its foliage is the Artemisia 'Powis Castle', a pretty silvery blue. Dale Booher and Lisa Stamm move their work sessions indoors, to contemplate not so much the border itself, but some five months' worth of notes about it. These tend to be the hardest months for a team like Ms. Stamm and Mr. Booher, not because of the dreary weather, but because the longer they are locked indoors, the more time they have to devise new schemes they cannot possibly do without. So it is that even in the dead of winter, the garden is growing.

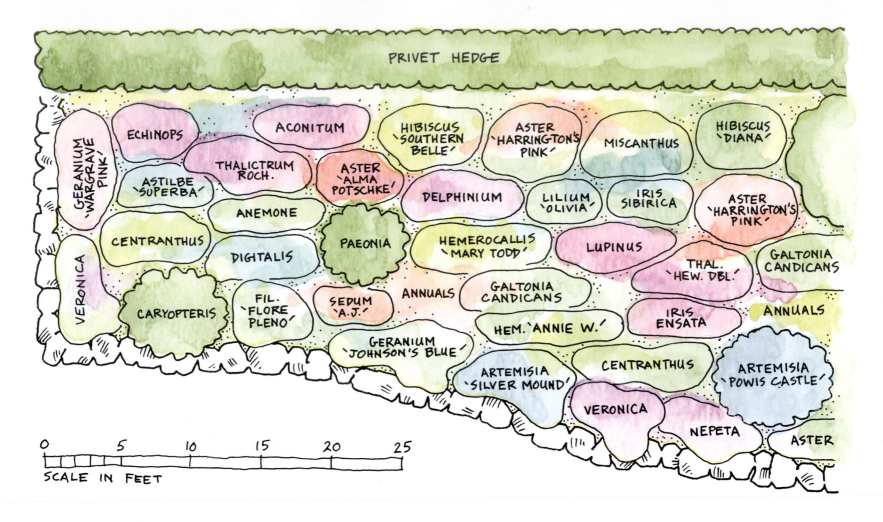

PRIVET HEDGE

GERANIUM 'WARGRAVE PINK'

ECHINOPS

ACONITUM

HIBISCUS 'SOUTHERN BELLE'

ASTER 'HARRINGTON'S PINK'

MISCANTHUS

HIBISCUS 'DIANA'

THALICTRUM ROCH.

ASTILBE 'SUPERBA'

ASTER 'ALMA POTSCHKE'

DELPHINIUM

LILIUM 'OLIVIA'

IRIS SIBIRICA

ASTER 'HARRINGTON'S PINK'

ANEMONE

CENTRANTHUS

PAEONIA

HEMEROCALLIS 'MARY TODD'

LUPINUS

GALTONIA CANDICANS

VERONICA

DIGITALIS

THAL. HEW. DBL.

CARYOPTERIS

FIL. 'FLORE PLENO'

SEDUM 'A.J.'

ANNUALS

GALTONIA CANDICANS

IRIS ENSATA

ANNUALS

HEM. 'ANNIE W.'

GERANIUM 'JOHNSON'S BLUE'

CENTRANTHUS

ARTEMISIA 'SILVER MOUND'

ARTEMISIA 'POWIS CASTLE'

VERONICA

NEPETA

ASTER

0   5   10   15   20   25

SCALE IN FEET

"The Homestead" Garden of Lisa Stamm and Dale Booher Shelter Island, New York

SITE: Full sun

SOIL: Slightly acid, sandy loam

ZONE: 7a

PLANT LIST

PERENNIALS

Aconitum sparksii *Monkshood*

Anemone x hybrida 'Honorine Jobert' *Japanese anemone*

Artemisia 'Powis Castle' and 'Silver Mound'

Aster 'Alma Potschke', 'Coombe Violet', 'Harrington's Pink', 'Romany', and 'Summer Sunshine'

Astilbe 'Peach Blossom'

A. taquetti 'Superba'

Campanula persicifolia *Willow bellflower*

Caryopteris

Centranthus ruber *Red valerian*

Delphinium 'Bluebird'

Digitalis 'Excelsior' hybrids *Foxglove*

Echinops ritro *Small globe thistle*

Filipendula rubra 'Venusta' *Meadowsweet*

F. vulgaris 'Flore Pleno' (F. hexapetala) *Dropwort*

Galtonia candicans

Geranium 'Johnson's Blue' and 'Wargrave Pink'

G. sanguineum var. prostratum (G. lancastriense) *Cranesbill*

Helianthus salicifolius

Hemerocallis 'Annie Welch' and 'Mary Todd' *Daylily*

Hibiscus syriacus 'Diana' and 'Southern Belle' *Rose of Sharon*

Iris ensata 'Haku Botan' *Japanese iris*

I. sibirica 'Caesar's Brother' *Siberian iris*

Lilium 'Olivia'

Lupinus 'Russell Strain'

Lythrum virgatum 'Morden Pink' *Loosestrife*

Miscanthus sinensis 'Gracillimus'

Monarda 'Snow White' *Bee balm, Oswego tea*

Nepeta mussinii *Catmint*

Paeonia lactiflora 'Sarah Bernhardt' *Peony*

Phlox paniculata 'Starfire' *Garden phlox*

Sedum cauticolum

S. purpureum 'Autumn Joy' *Stonecrop*

Stachys byzantina (S. lanata) *Lamb's-ears*

Thalictrum 'Hewitt's Double'

T. rochebrunianum *Meadow rue*

Veronica latifolia 'Crater Lake Blue'

Vitex

ANNUALS AS FILLERS

Abelmoschus manihot

Cleome 'Helen Campbell'

Euphorbia marginata *Snow-on-the-mountain*

Helianthus annuus 'Italian White' *Sunflower*

Nicotiana sylvestris *Flowering tobacco*

Pentas white *Star-cluster*

Salvia 'Indigo Spires'

S. leucantha *Mexican bush sage*

Verbena bonariensis *Vervain*

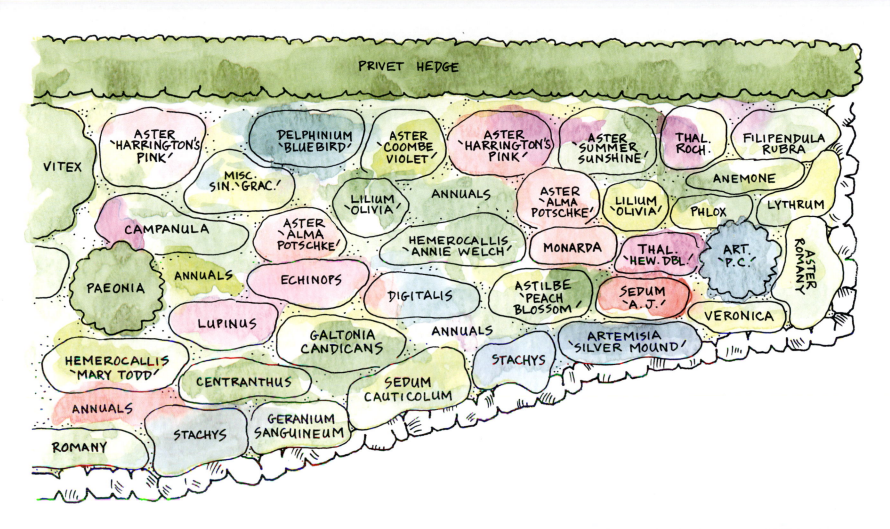

PRIVET HEDGE

ASTER 'HARRINGTON'S PINK'

DELPHINIUM 'BLUEBIRD'

ASTER 'COOMBE VIOLET'

ASTER 'HARRINGTON'S PINK'

ASTER 'SUMMER SUNSHINE'

THAL. ROCH.

FILIPENDULA RUBRA

VITEX

MISC. SIN. 'GRAC.'

LILIUM 'OLIVIA'

ANNUALS

ASTER 'ALMA POTSCHKE'

LILIUM 'OLIVIA'

ANEMONE

PHLOX

LYTHRUM

CAMPANULA

ASTER 'ALMA POTSCHKE'

HEMEROCALLIS 'ANNIE WELCH'

MONARDA

THAL. 'HEW. DBL.'

ART. 'P.C.'

ASTER ROMANY

PAEONIA

ANNUALS

ECHINOPS

DIGITALIS

ASTILBE 'PEACH BLOSSOM'

SEDUM 'A. J.'

VERONICA

LUPINUS

GALTONIA CANDICANS

ANNUALS

ARTEMISIA 'SILVER MOUND'

HEMEROCALLIS 'MARY TODD'

CENTRANTHUS

SEDUM CAUTICOLUM

STACHYS

ANNUALS

GERANIUM SANGUINEUM

ROMANY

STACHYS

N

As the peony 'Sarah Bernhardt' finishes blooming, the surrounding lilies, hollyhocks, and Thalictrum 'Hewitt's Double' come into flower, providing on-going interest.

The Neighborly Border

Several years ago, friends and neighbors of Randy Harelson and Richard Gibbs received excited phone calls: the Datura — that huge white morning-glorylike flower made immortal by the Georgia O'Keeffe painting — was in bloom in a large pot on their front doorstep. All were urged to come over and see. To get to it, friends had to walk through a border that pours from the front of the house in a frenzy of blossoms and stops only inches from the narrow street. This much enthusiasm, from both the plants and their cultivators, might seem strange to the uninitiated, but the Harelson-Gibbs neighborhood is well used to this kind of flora-mania.

The property's previous owner had also been an avid gardener, who, according to Randy

The Harelson-Gibbs front border, stretching from the house to the street, combines cultivated species, such as the espaliered Pyracantha, with wild drop-ins, including Queen-Anne's-lace (Daucus carota), which stands behind the Thalictrum.

Harelson, grew a night-blooming cereus in the bay window at the front of the house. When this weird-looking plant bloomed — something it does rarely but magnificently — he would place it on a table at the end of his front walk, carry out a lamp, and illuminate the plant's nocturnal flowering for all to see.

That owner's front yard also tended to be lush and exuberant. When Mr. Harelson and Mr. Gibbs bought the house in 1977, they lived with the border for about a year before concluding that the entire property was so wild that they could afford to neaten up the front. They pulled out the roses, peonies, black-eyed Susans, and orange daylilies that tumbled everywhere, and put a Santolina hedge across the front. Behind that they planted great quantities of a single variety of annual, changing their selection from year to year. They had Gomphrena, marigolds, Ageratum, and tuberous begonias, all of which they loved. Annuals gave the border glorious color and a certain continuity, but after a while they began

to find the single-species border far too unadventurous.

Over time, the front border evolved back into a familiar jumble of flowers, and by the end of ten years, it had gone full circle — from wild, to orderly, and back to wild again. The cottage's previous owner had had a vigorous foundation planting of Taxus that was so tall it framed the casement windows on the ground floor. In fact, Mr. Gibbs and Mr. Harelson discovered their bluestone path's existence only when they pulled out the huge bushes. But they liked the idea of an evergreen up against the house, so they planted a Boxwood hedge to cap the fieldstone wall, and a Pyracantha, which they espaliered up the wall and trained around the windows.

By the time the Pyracantha had achieved almost the full height of the Taxus it replaced, the plants that the cottage's prior owner had grown were back in the border again, with the exception of the daylilies. These, Mr. Harelson notes, are bound to be reintroduced soon.

Every spring, seedlings and perennial divisions that can't be used are potted up for the Harelson-Gibbs plant sale, which Randy Harelson refers to as their version of a tag sale, so offspring of their border's plants dot the community. At one of their first sales, Mr. Harelson recalls, a woman who had just moved to the neighborhood bought enough plants to stock her garden. A few years later she returned with a present, urging them to disregard the fact that the plant wasn't much to look at, for the flowers, she promised, would more than make up for it.

Randy Harelson took her at her word and planted the little clump of unpromising-looking foliage in his back border. Then he more or less forgot about it, until one summer's evening when he happened to look out the window while he was talking on the telephone. Where there had been foliage in the fading light, there was now a bright spot of yellow. In moments, there was another. "Excuse me," he told his surprised listener, "I've got to see what's happening in my garden," and raced outside. As he stood there, the flowers of the little plant unfurled, "just like a lady opening a fan." The

neighborhood was duly notified, of course, and the next night everyone came to watch the yellow flowers open, which happens, Mr. Harelson says, in a matter of two or three seconds. The plant is a kind of Oenothera (evening primrose), but Mr. Harelson hasn't yet been able to ascertain which species it is. In the meantime, it causes untold delight, and if he is able to get a division of it, he plans to move some into the front border where more people can see it.

The front border seems to provide at least one special thrill for the neighborhood each year. Once it was a stand of Delphinium, bought from a greenhouse in early spring and transplanted into the border. They grew upwards of six feet tall, and, Mr. Harelson says, "people driving by would screech their tires" trying to stop and look. But that was his sole success with plants of the genus, which he thinks is because the border has since become too crowded for their liking.

Another traffic-stopper is an annual ornamental bean called Dolichos lablab, or the Hyacinth Bean, which Mr. Harelson received in a way typical of many gardening transactions. He was visiting New Orleans when a friend who is the horticulturist for the city's parks pulled a bean pod off a plant and handed it to him. The pod went into a pocket, and resurfaced a year later when he was wearing the same jacket. He planted the seeds in pots, and within two days, Mr. Harelson remembers with something near horror, they were six inches tall. "But then," he says, "they stopped growing like that, and stayed reasonable." Transplanted into the garden, they formed a red-stemmed vine, with a pinkish-purple beanlike flower. But the real treat, according to Mr. Harelson, comes when they produce their brilliant, deep-purple seedpods.

Not all of the Harelson imports are complete successes with the neighborhood. He put some Verbascum thapsus — the common mullein that grows wild in dry fields — right in the front of the border. "They really made a stir," he recalls. "People would come by and say, 'Rip those out. They're weeds!'" The Verbascum is a biennial, so if one year is bad for seeds or seedlings, two years later there will be few or no flowering plants. This had happened recently, for the year we photographed, the garden had but one Verbascum.

ABOVE: *Feverfew (Chrysanthemum parthenium), Rudbeckias 'Goldquelle' and 'Goldsturm', and the prolific rose 'Seafoam' clamber around and over the fence. Delphinium and pink lilies are closer to the house.* OPPOSITE: *In early July, the bright-magenta Lychnis coronaria 'Abbotswood Rose', a short-lived perennial that self-seeds readily, lines the path.*

I suspect, however, that if there is no improvement next year, Mr. Harelson will get permission to venture out into a neighboring field and restock. The same can be said for his population of Queen-Anne's-lace, a plant that arrived in the border on its own and has been allowed to stay and establish itself.

Other plants that reseed are Cosmos; the Datura, which has spread from its pot to form a stand five feet wide in the bluestone walk; and, to a lesser degree, Cleome. All of this adds up to a sort of surprise garden, for allowing everything to reseed itself means giving up control over what will come up, or where. It also means a lot of thinning out and moving around of tiny seedlings, and that weeding can be done only by hand — never by hoe. In addition, the Buddleia has to be deadheaded almost daily so that it will carry on blooming all summer, and many of the other plants need recurrent deadheading. Randy Harelson reckons that the border takes six to seven hours of his time each week — not exactly a low-maintenance garden — but he doesn't complain. The garden is for the neighborhood and for the butterflies, he claims, and while he works, members of both groups come by. They all let him know what they like, and the response to date has been gratifying.

LEFT: *Mr. Harelson and Mr. Gibbs have a private border behind the house, where Heliopsis and Veronica spicata 'Blue Charm' bloom together in early July.*

OPPOSITE: *One of the few plants in the garden that invariably require staking, the border's tiger lilies (Lilium tigrinum) flower on five- to six-foot-tall stems in mid-July.*

SITE: Morning sun

SOIL: Neutral, sandy loam

ZONE: 7a

PLANT LIST

PERENNIALS

Alcea rosea, mixed pink
   Hollyhock
Alchemilla mollis *Lady's-mantle*
Aster x frikartii
Buddleia davidii *Butterfly bush*
Campanula, blue
Centaurea montana
   Mountain bluet
Cerastium tomentosum
   Snow-in-summer
Chrysanthemum x
   morifolium
   Spoon chrysanthemum
C. parthenium (Matricaria)
   Feverfew
Clematis paniculata
   Sweet autumn clematis
Delphinium 'Pacific Giant'
Digitalis grandiflora (D. lutea)
   Yellow foxglove
D. 'Temple Bells'
Galium odoratum *Sweet woodruff*
Helianthus *Sungold sunflower*
Hosta plantaginea x 'Honey Bells'
Hydrangea macrophylla
   Lacecap, Hortensia
Iris ensata 'Ise' *Japanese iris*
I. x germanica, purple
   Bearded iris
Lamium, silver and white
   variegated evergreen
   Dead nettle
Lilium auratum 'Rubrum'
L. Connecticut Yankee strain
L. pink
L. tigrinum
Lychnis coronaria 'Abbotswood
   Rose' *Rose campion*
Mentha variegated *Mint*
Monarda didyma 'Croftway Pink'
   Bee balm, Oswego tea
Paeonia lactiflora, hot pink, pink
   with ruffled center, single
   pink, and single white *Peony*

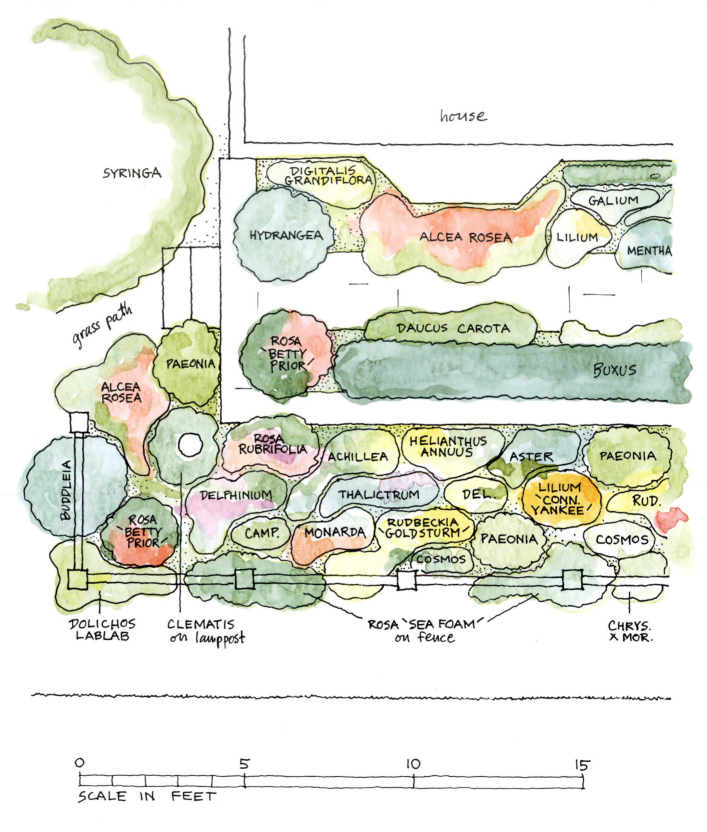

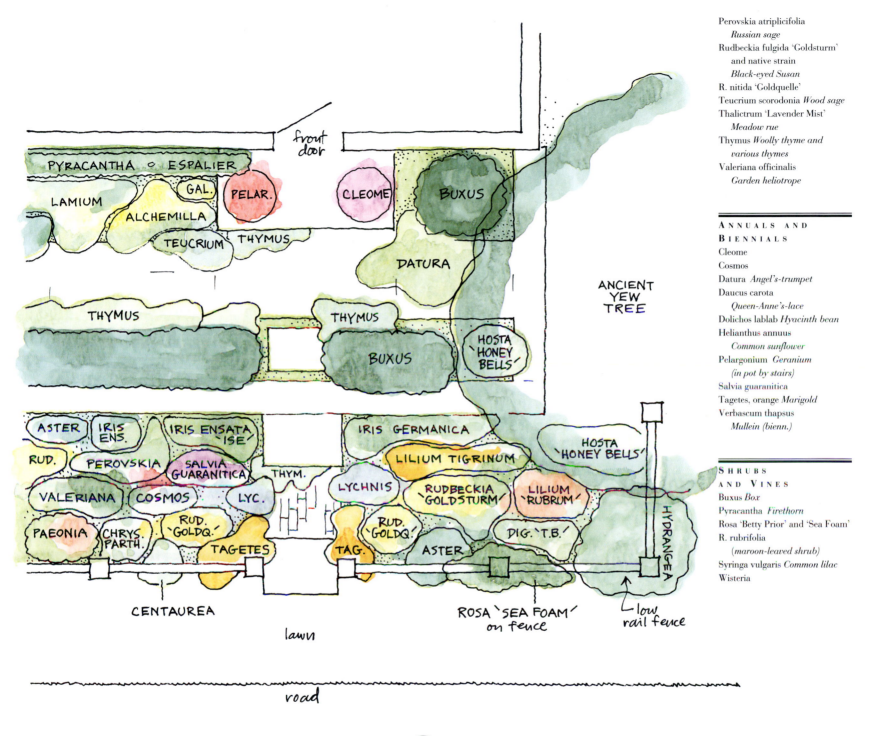

Perovskia atriplicifolia
   Russian sage
Rudbeckia fulgida 'Goldsturm'
   and native strain
   Black-eyed Susan
R. nitida 'Goldquelle'
Teucrium scorodonia *Wood sage*
Thalictrum 'Lavender Mist'
   Meadow rue
Thymus *Woolly thyme and
   various thymes*
Valeriana officinalis
   Garden heliotrope

ANNUALS AND
BIENNIALS
Cleome
Cosmos
Datura *Angel's-trumpet*
Daucus carota
   Queen-Anne's-lace
Dolichos lablab *Hyacinth bean*
Helianthus annuus
   Common sunflower
Pelargonium *Geranium
   (in pot by stairs)*
Salvia guaranitica
Tagetes, orange *Marigold*
Verbascum thapsus
   Mullein (bienn.)

SHRUBS
AND VINES
Buxus *Box*
Pyracantha *Firethorn*
Rosa 'Betty Prior' and 'Sea Foam'
R. rubrifolia
   (maroon-leaved shrub)
Syringa vulgaris *Common lilac*
Wisteria

PYRACANTHA ○ ESPALIER
LAMIUM
GAL.
ALCHEMILLA
PELAR.
CLEOME
BUXUS
front door
TEUCRIUM
THYMUS
DATURA
ANCIENT YEW TREE

THYMUS
THYMUS
BUXUS
HOSTA HONEY BELLS

ASTER
IRIS ENS.
IRIS ENSATA 'ISE'
IRIS GERMANICA
HOSTA HONEY BELLS
RUD.
PEROVSKIA
SALVIA GUARANITICA
THYM.
LILIUM TIGRINUM
VALERIANA
COSMOS
LYC.
LYCHNIS
RUDBECKIA GOLDSTURM
LILIUM RUBRUM
PAEONIA
CHRYS. PARTH.
RUD. GOLDQ.
RUD. GOLDQ
DIG. T.B.
TAGETES
TAG.
ASTER
HYDRANGEA

CENTAUREA
ROSA 'SEA FOAM' on fence
low rail fence

lawn

road

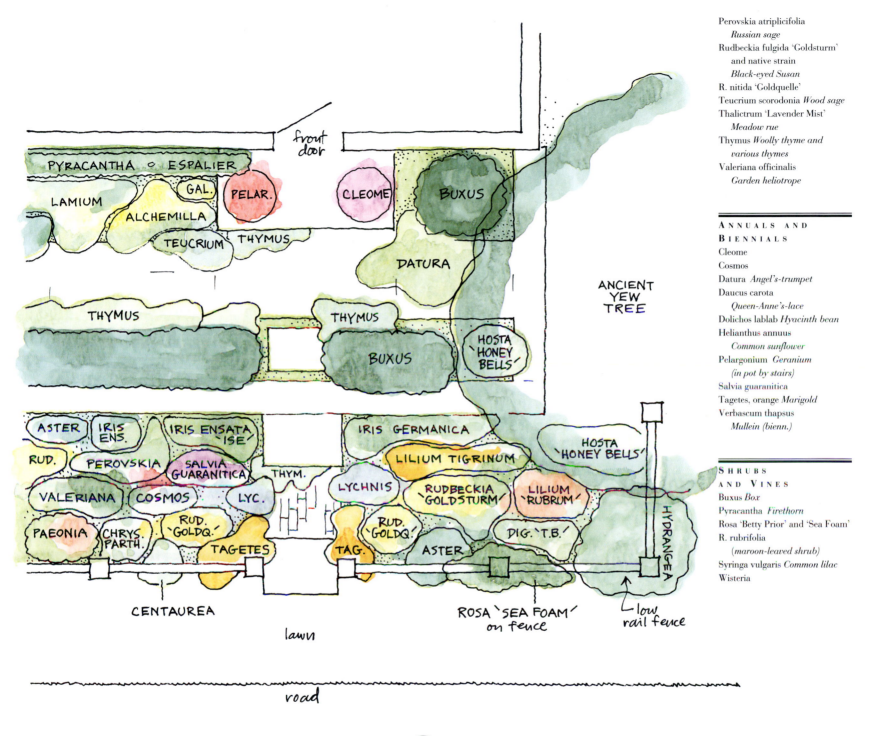

N →

Working with a View

For a landscape designer, a view can be exhilarating or exasperating, an element to be incorporated into an overall scheme or screened out with something like a hedge. When professional garden designer Edwina von Gal saw the beautiful valley that dominates the outlook from most of this property, she knew she wanted to make the most of it. This choice made her task more complex; instead of composing a picture against an unvarying green backdrop, she had to make the borders work with — and, to a degree, stand out against — the landscape.

Diana Burroughs and Jason McCoy, the garden's owners, had given only two edicts at the beginning of the project: that they wanted peonies, and that they would use the house in spring, early summer, and fall, but not much in August. Apart from that, Mrs. von Gal was on her own. For spring she chose bright, cheerful flowers such as dark-pink peonies; red, yellow, and blue lupines; lime-green Alchemilla; and lavender Nepeta — all to catch the eye and warm the spir-

it after a long cold winter. But for summer she opted for low-keyed, textural plants that would blend into the view. For fall the colors liven up again, with the blooms of the reddish-plum Hemerocallis 'Wild Heart', the raspberry-red and pink flowers of two Sedums ('Brilliant' and 'Autumn Joy'), pink Lythrum, and, last of all to open, the white clouds of Boltonia.

Running through all the seasons is a basic color scheme of blue, chartreuse, and blue-yellow. Helictotrichon (blue oat grass) has fountains of frosty-blue leaves from spring until fall, and Stachys byzantina makes a carpet of felt-covered leaves of a paler color for the same long season. More early silvery-blue foliage comes from Achillea 'Moonshine', which tops itself off with greenish-yellow flowers in summer. Alchemilla holds its chartreuse spring flowers into July, and its

Lupines, which sulk in the warm, humid summers of many American gardens, are the mainstay of this border's June show.

In June, the border is bright with lupines, peonies, Alchemilla, Salvia 'East Friesland', and the silvery foliage of Stachys byzantina.

bluish leaves remain through fall. Coreopsis verticillata 'Moonbeam' produces acid-yellow flowers from June until severe frost cuts down the whole plant. The sedums' blue-green foliage shows all summer, topped with immature flower heads that only begin to ripen into their bright colors in August.

With these as a mainstay, other flowers and colors come and go through the seasons. Pinks (generally on the rose or blue side), lavenders, and purples predominate in spring and fall, whereas summer abounds with yellows. A few — but only a few — orangy-yellows appear in the summer daylily show, adding a lit-

tle zip to the borders without altering the generally serene composition. As a result, Mrs. von Gal achieves a subdued feeling for summer without relying on a theme that she calls "the same old silver and white." For spring and fall, she arranged for a bright show without having to dip heavily into the hot colors.

The garden's first winter killed all the Shasta daisies — not a surprise in a region as cold as this one, where temperatures often drop to twenty degrees below zero. But everything else pulled through magnificently, putting on a first-year show — as seen here — that would put many a more mature garden to shame.

One is tempted to believe that there is some secret to getting a border to look this good after only one year. But Mrs. von Gal quickly clarifies that it is no secret, just the archaic, labor-intensive practice that often falls prey to budget cuts: double digging. Mrs. von Gal makes sure that one foot, if not two or three, of the existing soil is tossed out and replaced with quality loam. She is equally stubborn about drainage, putting gravel and drainpipes at the bottom of all of the border trenches. "Otherwise," she says, "you're just building a very expensive bathtub." The garden has rewarded her for this extra care.

By summer, the border is subdued, with silver and blue foliage, the immature chartreuse flower heads of the Sedum, and a variety of yellow flowers.

RIGHT: *Helictotrichon holds its form and color from spring until, and often through, winter. Behind it blooms Hemerocallis 'Golden Gift'.*

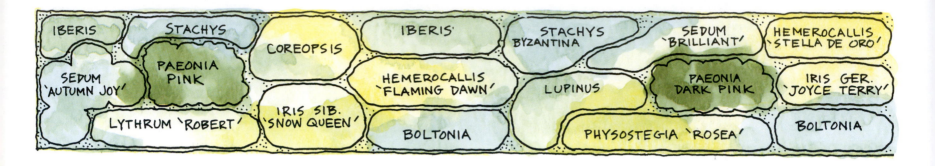

SCALE IN FEET

Garden of Jason
McCoy and
Diana Burroughs
Otsego County,
New York
Designed by
Edwina von Gal
SITE: Full sun
SOIL: Loam, slightly acid
ZONE: 4b

PLANT LIST

PERENNIALS

Achillea 'Moonshine' *Yarrow*
Alchemilla mollis *Lady's-mantle*
Boltonia asteroides 'Snowbank'
Chrysanthemum maximum
   Daisy chrysanthemum
Coreopsis verticillata
   'Moonbeam' *Tickseed*
Delphinium
Deschampsia caespitosa
   Tufted hair grass
Digitalis 'Giant Shirley'
Helictotrichon *Blue oat grass*

Hemerocallis 'Flaming Dawn'
   (cream, azalea pink), 'George
   Caleb Bingham' (deep rose
   pink), 'Golden Gift' (golden
   yellow), 'Heavenly Harp'
   (cream yellow with rose),
   'Stella de Oro' (bright yellow),
   'Tropic Tangerine' (tangerine
   orange), and 'Wild Heart'
   (reddish plum) *Daylily*
Hosta 'Royal Standard'
Iberis sempervirens *Candytuft*
Iris x germanica 'Beverly Sills'
   (pink), 'Deep Space' (dark
   blue), 'Joyce Terry' (cream
   yellow), and white
   Bearded iris

I. siberica 'Persimmon' (blue),
   'Snow Queen' (white), and
   dark purple *Siberian iris*
Liatris scariosa 'September Glory'
   Gay-feather
Lupinus of various colors
Lythrum virgatum 'Morden Pink'
   Loosestrife
L. salicaria 'Robert'
Nepeta *Catmint*
Paeonia, dark pink, light pink,
   and white *Peony*
Physostegia virginiana 'Rosea',
   'Summer Snow', and 'Vivid'
   Obedient plant

Salvia nemorosa
   'East Friesland' *Meadow sage*
Sedum spectabile 'Brilliant'
   Stonecrop
S. purpureum 'Autumn Joy'
   Stonecrop
Stachys byzantina (S. lanata)
   Lamb's-ears

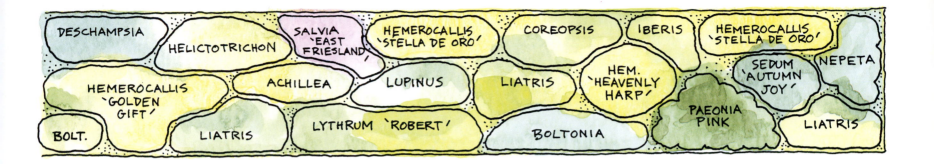

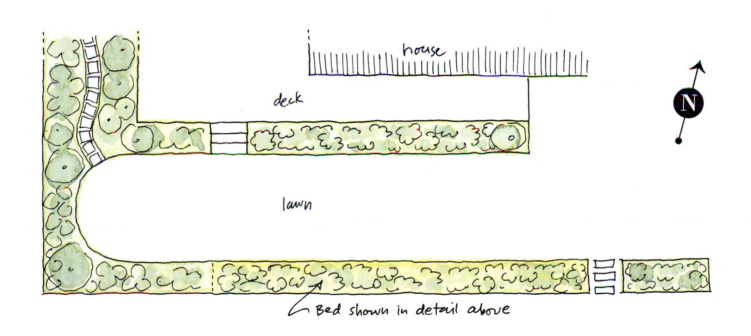

Bed shown in detail above

CHAPTER NINE

Spring in High Summer

Ginny Purviance's border in late July seduces visitors with its softness. High summer is a time most of us expect some fairly strong colors in a garden, but here, from end to end, the border is dappled with pink, lavender, and pale-blue flowers, and the pale green that makes you think of tender new growth. Before you know it, you've been lulled into imagining it's early June, so it's quite a shock to walk around the house and see Mrs. Purviance's other borders, which are laden with orange, red, and yellow.

Having grown up at the heels of two gardening grandmothers, one of whom had a garden designed by the preeminent American landscape architect Beatrix Farrand, Mrs. Purviance found

In the first week of July, when you expect to see some hot colors in a garden, the Purviance border still looks spring-like, with the pale blue-green and chartreuse of Sedum and Alchemilla, pink and white Dianthus x allwoodii, blue Iris kaempferi, and creamy-white Astilbe 'Bridal Veil'.

her affinity for plants and design predestined. Her mother also had what Mrs. Purviance recalls as "a truly sublime garden," with terraces, pools, and fountains, enclosed by brick walls. So it was inevitable that when she and her family first moved to this house south of Providence in 1977, Ginny Purviance immediately began to transform "a stone wall, a crab apple tree, a lot of Solomon's-seal, a rock, and a piece of fence" into a border. Mrs. Purviance recalls that the area also contained "three *beautiful* Baptisias. They were about five feet tall. I was such a neophyte that I'd never seen a Baptisia before." Novice or not, she knew enough to save them.

To the Baptisias she added, over the years, a variety of different plant combinations, always steering clear of hot colors. Her spring-in-mid-summer color scheme relies on the pale greens of the buds and leaves of Sedum purpureum 'Autumn Joy', the annual Nicotiana alata 'Lime Sherbet', and the old chartreuse standby, Alchemilla mollis. Into that she mixes white, with Asiatic

LEFT: *Achillea 'Rose Queen' Lilium 'Candlelight', and Liatris 'Kobold' bloom in the front of the border.*

OPPOSITE: *By mid-July, the border's Filipendula rubra 'Venusta' Sidalcea, and petunias are full of pink blossoms, while canary grass (Phalaris arundinacera) adds more cream and light green. In the front of the border, an old tree stump is camouflaged with a selection of potted plants.*

Even at the end of July, the border maintains its predominantly pale green and pink color scheme. Here, Lunaria annua and Monarda didyma 'Croftway Pink' bloom together.

lilies, Physostegia virginiana 'Alba', Aruncus dioicus, and Dianthus x allwoodii. Pink comes in the form of Achillea millefolium, Malva moschata, and Sidalcea malviflora, while Liatris spicata 'Kobold', Nepeta mussinii 'Dropmore', and Platycodon grandiflorus contribute patches of lavender.

Mrs. Purviance, who ran a flower-arranging business that kept her "and a fleet of minions tending plants all over Newport," turned her attention to the outdoors in 1982, when she entered the Master's program in landscape design at Radcliffe. As her experience broadened, so did her seventy-foot-long border, which began life at four feet wide and by 1989 had spread to ten. (Since we photographed the border, Mrs. Purviance has doubled its breadth to twenty feet.)

Although she has continually made the border bigger, she hasn't aggrandized it. All her plants tend to be "the most commonly available cultivars," the idea being to keep the border, like her house, "simple and comfortable." This refers to both visual and operational aspects. Mrs. Purviance declines to take her border too seriously, subjecting it to whims — her garden notes for June 9, 1988, refer to "a binge at McGourty's" (Hillside Gardens in Norfolk, Connecticut) that resulted in a number of plants she didn't need but found room for — and to spur-of-the-moment decisions. Her Filipendula rubra 'Venusta', which she says reminds her of pink cotton candy, came to the border because she saw some on the roadside, hanging over a post-and-rail fence, and, with the owner's blessing, took a clump home. Her beloved pink Achillea millefolium 'Cerise Queen' returned with her from a visit to a friend's herb farm.

The only tangible asset Ginny Purviance has from any of her family's gardens is some pale-yellow Thalictrum that came from the Farrand-designed border of her grandmother; handed down by her mother, a descendant of it now grows in a red, orange, and yellow border near Mrs. Purviance's driveway. Still, the fact that she has a garden to grow it in tells of a passion that has been with her since childhood, which Ginny Purviance feels is legacy enough.

Malva moschata and the similar but brighter Sidalcea malviflora 'Elsie Heugh' flank Nicotiana alata 'Lime Sherbet', blue Platycodon grandiflorus, wine-red Allium sphaerocephalum, and the small red-centered white annual Chrysanthemum 'Court Jester'. In the front is Nepeta mussinii.

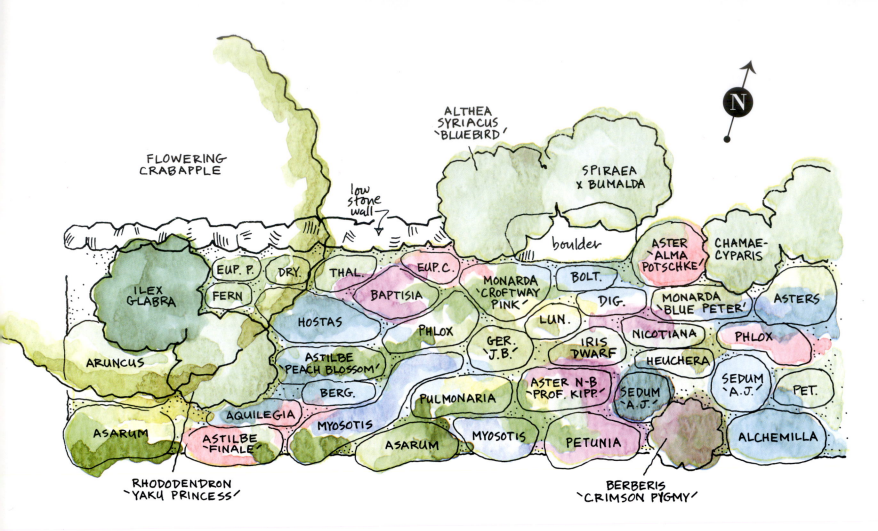

Labels on map (image):

FLOWERING CRABAPPLE

ALTHEA SYRIACUS 'BLUEBIRD'

SPIRAEA x BUMALDA

N

low stone wall

boulder

EUP. P. · DRY. · THAL. · EUP. C.

FERN

ILEX GLABRA

HOSTAS

BAPTISIA

MONARDA 'CROFTWAY PINK'

BOLT.

ASTER 'ALMA POTSCHKE'

CHAMAE-CYPARIS

DIG.

MONARDA 'BLUE PETER'

ASTERS

PHLOX

LUN.

NICOTIANA

PHLOX

ARUNCUS

GER. J.B.

IRIS DWARF

HEUCHERA

ASTILBE 'PEACH BLOSSOM'

BERG.

PULMONARIA

ASTER N-B PROF. KIPP.

SEDUM 'A.J.'

SEDUM 'A.J.'

PET.

AQUILEGIA

MYOSOTIS

ASARUM

ASTILBE 'FINALE'

ASARUM

MYOSOTIS

PETUNIA

ALCHEMILLA

RHODODENDRON 'YAKU PRINCESS'

BERBERIS 'CRIMSON PYGMY'

Border of Virginia P. Purviance, Middletown, Rhode Island

SITE: Sunny, with patches of light shade

SOIL: Slightly acid sandy loam

ZONE: 7a

PLANT LIST

PERENNIALS

Achillea millefolium 'Cerise Queen' *Yarrow*

Alchemilla mollis *Lady's-mantle*

Allium sphaerocephalum *Round-headed garlic*

Aquilegia x hybrida 'McKana Hybrid' *Columbine*

Aruncus dioicus *Goatsbeard*

Asarum canadense *Wild ginger*

Aster 'Alma Potschke'

A. x frikartii

A. novae-angliae 'Alice Haslam', 'Mt. Everest', and wild blue

A. novi-belgii 'Prof. Kippenburg'

Astilbe x arendsii 'Bridal Veil' and 'Peachblossom'

A. 'Fanal' and 'Finale'

Baptisia australis *False indigo*

Bergenia cordifolia 'Morninglight'

Boltonia asteroides 'Snowbank'

Crambe cordifolia *Colewort*

Dianthus x allwoodii

Digitalis purpurea 'Excelsior' *Foxglove*

Dryopteris *Fern*

Eupatorium coelestinum *Mist flower, Hardy ageratum*

E. purpureum *Joe-Pye weed*

Filipendula albicans

F. rubra 'Venusta' *Queen-of-the-prairie*

Geranium 'Johnson's Blue' and 'Magnificum' *Cranesbill*

Gillenia trifoliata *Bowman's-root*

Heuchera sanguinea 'Chatterbox' *Alumroot, Coralbells*

Hosta 'Blue Moon' and 'Honeybells'

H. sieboldiana

Iris, dwarf bearded white

I. x germanica 'Pride of Ireland' *Bearded iris*

I. ensata 'Shadow' *Japanese iris*

Liatris spicata 'Kobold' *Gay-feather*

Lilium 'Candlelight' (Asiatic)

Lunaria annua *Money plant*

Lupinus, pink

Lychnis coronaria *Rose campion*

Malva moschata *Musk mallow*

Monarda didyma 'Blue Peter' and 'Croftway Pink' *Bee balm, Oswego tea*

Myosotis scorpioides *Forget-me-not*

Nepeta mussinii 'Dropmore' *Catmint*

Osmunda claytoniana *Fern*

Phalaris arundinacea *Canary grass*

Phlox paniculata, pink and white *Garden phlox*

Physostegia virginiana 'Alba' *Obedient plant*

Platycodon grandiflorus *Balloon flower*

Polygonatum canaliculatum *Solomon's-seal*

Pulmonaria montana 'Salmon Glow' *Lungwort*

Salvia

Sanguinaria canadensis *Bloodroot*

Sedum purpureum 'Autumn Joy' and 'Vera Jameson' *Stonecrop*

S. 'Rosy Glow' *Stonecrop*

Sidalcea malviflora 'Elsie Heugh' *Checkerbloom*

Stachys byzantina (S. lanata) *Lamb's-ears*

Stephanandra incisa 'crispa' *Lace shrub*

Strobilanthes atropurpurea

Thalictrum rochebrunianum *Meadow rue*

Valeriana officinalis *Garden heliotrope*

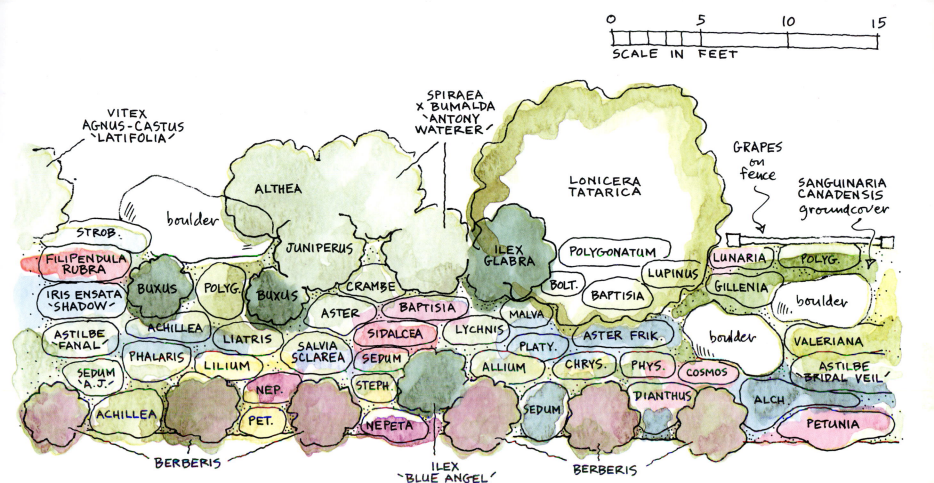

SCALE IN FEET

0   5   10   15

VITEX
AGNUS-CASTUS
'LATIFOLIA'

SPIRAEA
X BUMALDA
'ANTONY
WATERER'

GRAPES
on
fence

SANGUINARIA
CANADENSIS
groundcover

boulder

ALTHEA

JUNIPERUS

LONICERA
TATARICA

STROB.

ILEX
GLABRA

POLYGONATUM

LUNARIA

POLYG.

FILIPENDULA
RUBRA

BUXUS

POLYG.

BUXUS

CRAMBE

LUPINUS

GILLENIA

boulder

IRIS ENSATA
'SHADOW'

ASTER

BAPTISIA

BOLT.

BAPTISIA

ACHILLEA

SIDALCEA

LYCHNIS

MALVA

ASTER FRIK.

boulder

VALERIANA

ASTILBE
FANAL

LIATRIS

SALVIA
SCLAREA

SEDUM

PLATY.

PHALARIS

LILIUM

ALLIUM

CHRYS.

PHYS.

COSMOS

ASTILBE
'BRIDAL VEIL'

SEDUM
A.J.

STEPH.

DIANTHUS

ALCH.

NEP.

SEDUM

ACHILLEA

PET.

NEPETA

SEDUM

PETUNIA

BERBERIS

ILEX
'BLUE ANGEL'

BERBERIS

*A bench provides
visual interest and
occasional respite for
the weary gardener.*

Shifting Palette

The New York Botanical Garden in the Bronx, New York, has always been one of the best places to cruise around with a pad and pencil because it is a living catalog of possibilities; now that Lynden Miller is in charge of garden design, the perennial borders are becoming the place for color magic. After establishing a stretch of "cool" borders, Mrs. Miller focused on the areas she had decided to make "hot."

One flanks the stairs behind the Enid Haupt Conservatory. In late May 1990 it was filled with the silvery foliage and white buds of Achillea 'Moonshine'. At the edge was a large stand of Achillea 'Coronation Gold', its buds showing a hint of yellow. Laced into all this paleness, like chocolate swirled through milk, was an S-curve of bluish-eggplant-colored Salvia 'East Friesland', also in bud. Two weeks later the border had erupted with a group of Kniphofia that glowed like the red-hot pokers they are commonly called. In mid-July, the bank behind the border was filled with yellow daylilies, and toward the front a large stand of Crocosmia 'Lucifer' blazed in strong reddish orange. Their arching wands were sandwiched between an old pine tree and the purple Prunus x cistena at the back and Achillea 'Coronation Gold' in front. This combination pleased Mrs. Miller enormously.

Less satisfactory were large clumps of pink Echinacea and a nearby drift of palest pink Oenothera, leftovers from a cooler color scheme. The Echinacea, Mrs. Miller said, "had its head chopped off, and it will be moved in the fall." The Oenothera was destined for the same fate. Contemplating what might replace them, Mrs. Miller ran through some possibilities. Dahlia 'Bishop of Llandaff', which has scarlet flowers and purple foliage, was mentioned, and she mused about

A mixed-color border is transformed to "hot" colors. The mid-July flowering Achillea 'Coronation Gold' in the foreground and Crocosmia 'Lucifer' behind it will remain. Still due for removal, however, are the cooler pink Echinacea, the creamy-plumed Macleaya, and the white Orlaya.

purple-leaved shrubs. Another candidate was Salvia coccinea — purple-leaved with small scarlet flowers, and grown in these latitudes as an annual.

Finally, Mrs. Miller decided to plant the annual Papaver rhoeas, using a variety that is off-white with a crimson edge. That would take care of spring, and for summer she would put in the Salvia coccinea.

To Lynden Miller, the border's transitional state is evident, and colors that don't fall into the "hot" category are bothersome; but someone unaware of her plans sees only a pretty, mixed border. Mrs. Miller copes with the changeover period decisively: she beheads off-color flowers so they won't be apparent, and removes and replants as swiftly as possible. A year later nobody will know that this area was ever anything but "hot."

ABOVE: *No hot color scheme would be complete without the aptly named Crocomsia 'Lucifer'.*
OPPOSITE: *In late June, the color scheme looks decidedly cool. Achillea 'Moonshine' has just opened, 'Coronation Gold' is green and white and the purple Salvia appears almost lavender.*

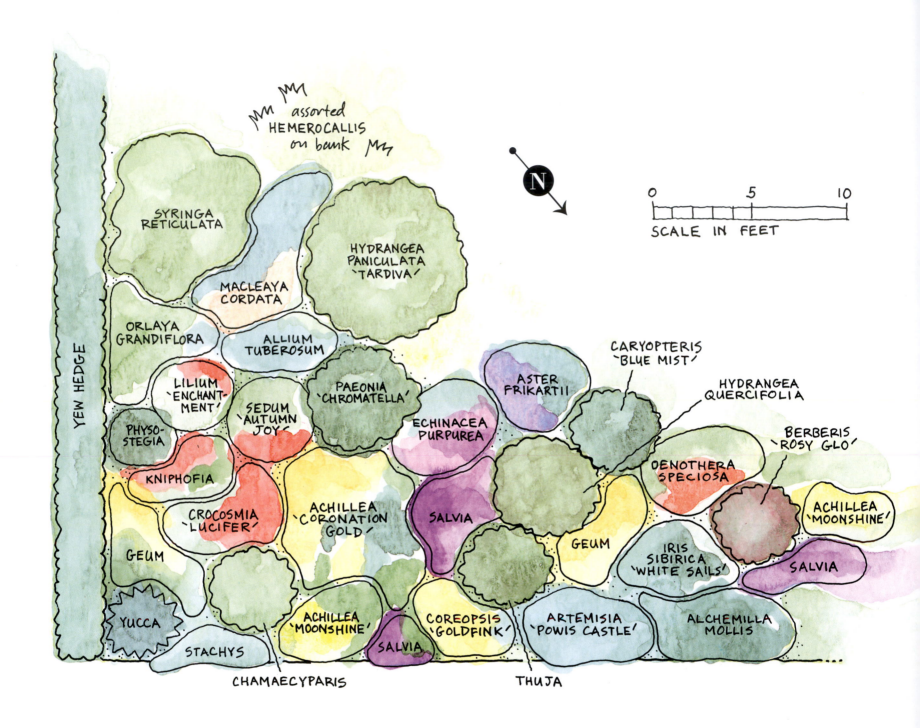

assorted
HEMEROCALLIS
on bank

N

0   5   10

SCALE IN FEET

YEW HEDGE

SYRINGA
RETICULATA

HYDRANGEA
PANICULATA
'TARDIVA'

MACLEAYA
CORDATA

ORLAYA
GRANDIFLORA

ALLIUM
TUBEROSUM

CARYOPTERIS
'BLUE MIST'

HYDRANGEA
QUERCIFOLIA

LILIUM
'ENCHANT-
MENT'

PAEONIA
'CHROMATELLA'

ASTER
FRIKARTII

SEDUM
AUTUMN
JOY'

ECHINACEA
PURPUREA

BERBERIS
'ROSY GLO'

PHYSO-
STEGIA

OENOTHERA
SPECIOSA

KNIPHOFIA

ACHILLEA
'MOONSHINE'

CROCOSMIA
'LUCIFER'

ACHILLEA
'CORONATION
GOLD'

SALVIA

GEUM

IRIS
SIBIRICA
'WHITE SAILS'

SALVIA

GEUM

YUCCA

ACHILLEA
'MOONSHINE'

SALVIA

COREOPSIS
'GOLDFINK'

ARTEMISIA
'POWIS CASTLE'

ALCHEMILLA
MOLLIS

STACHYS

CHAMAECYPARIS

THUJA

*The New York
Botanical Garden
"Hot" Section of
Perennial Borders
Designed by
Lynden B. Miller*

SITE: Full sun

SOIL: Slightly acid loam

ZONE: 7a

PLANT LIST

PERENNIALS

Achillea 'Coronation Gold' and
  'Moonshine' *Yarrow*
Alchemilla mollis *Lady's-mantle*
Allium tuberosum
Artemisia 'Powis Castle'
Aster x frikartii
Caryopteris x clandonensis
  'Blue Mist'
Coreopsis grandiflora 'Goldfink'
  Tickseed
Crocosmia 'Lucifer'
Echinacea purpurea
  Coneflower

Geum quellyon 'Lady
  Strathmore'
Hemerocallis vars. *Daylily*
Iris sibirica 'White Sails'
  Siberian iris
Kniphofia caulescens
  Red-hot-poker
Lilium 'Enchantment'
Oenothera speciosa
  Evening primrose
Physostegia virginiana 'Summer
  Snow' *Obedient plant*
Salvia 'East Friesland'
Sedum purpureum 'Autumn Joy'
  Stonecrop
Stachys byzantina (S. lanata)
  Lamb's-ears
Yucca filamentosa

ANNUALS AND BIENNIALS

Orlaya grandiflora

SHRUBS

Berberis thunbergii atropurpurea
  'Rosy Glo' *Barberry*
Chamaecyparis pisifera 'Filifera
  Aurea' *False cypress*
Hydrangea paniculata
  'Tardiva'
H. quercifolia
  Oak-leaf hydrangea
Paeonia suffruticosa
  'Chromatella'
Syringa reticulata var. reticulata
  Japanese tree lilac
Thuja occidentalis 'Ericoides'
  American arborvitae

*Often used in cooler
color schemes, the
Smoke bush, Cotinus
coggygria 'Purpureus',
in the back of the bor-
der is a marvelous foil
to the boldly colored
Achillea and Crocosmia.*

At a Distance

There are two points that Lisa Stamm makes when discussing the border she designed for a client in New York's northern Westchester County. The first is that at 112 feet long and 9 wide, it is large. The second is that it is a good distance from the house — your eye must traverse nearly a hundred feet of lawn and a swimming pool before reaching the border — and far from any well-traveled paths.

Consequently, the border is "not one of those that you walk right by several times a day," Ms. Stamm says, "so I tried to give it strong form rather than intimate detail." As the border underlies the view that the owners see from most windows of their house, she banked the soil beneath it so that the back is about eighteen inches higher than the front. Doing this not only made the border itself seem wider and more solid, but accentuated the composition within.

Lisa Stamm relies on big clumps throughout, and the repetition of certain plants, such as Nepeta mussinii or Miscanthus sinensis 'Gracil-

limus', to give the large design some continuity. Otherwise, she feels, "the border just fragments. When you see a design without continuity, it makes you think of pieces of a puzzle all shaken around in their box."

With a main flowering period of July through September, one of the special joys of this border occurs just as it begins. The Delphinium elatum 'Pacific' hybrids have been reliably perennial in the garden for several years, something that is rare in the hot, humid summers so typical of the region. Lisa Stamm attributes this to the garden's fortuitous hilltop position — there is almost always a cool breeze blowing, especially at night.

The only guidelines given to Ms. Stamm by the owners were that they loved blue, pink, and

Because this is an enormous border, usually seen from across a broad expanse of lawn, designer Lisa Stamm used huge clumps of perennials. To retain a sense of romance, she avoided architectural plants such as columnar evergreens and stayed with soft, mound-forming plants.

RIGHT: *Delphinium,
although generally such
a high-maintenance
plant in this area that it
is treated as an annual, if
used at all, thrives in this
garden. Ms. Stamm
thinks the reason is a
combination of good
drainage, rich soil, and
the relatively cool nights
that the hilltop position
provides.* FAR RIGHT:
*To keep such a large bor-
der cohesive, the designer
used some plants repeat-
edly throughout its
length. Large clumps of
Artemisia 'Powis Castle'
were planted in four
places along the front of
the border, two of which
can be seen here. Sedum
'Autumn Joy' is also used
four times, and yellow
and peach varieties of
Hemerocallis appear
throughout.*

white, and that they preferred she steer clear of too much yellow. So the border has no systematic color scheme, no rainbowlike parade of hues from one end to the other. As this border is most often seen head on, that sort of color progression might not have worked well anyway. Instead, Ms. Stamm dabbed her colors here and there as she felt they looked best, an approach that can be much harder.

Repeating plants gives the border a nice sense of rhythm, but her success in this venture is also due to her use of plants that form mounds, in or out of flower, which she arranges in large groups. With repetition of shapes and species as a framework, Lisa Stamm doesn't need to use blocks of related color to hold down her design. As she says, "When you have lots of different plants and colors everywhere, it can be intoxicating, but it is also exhausting to look at. I want my designs to be restful."

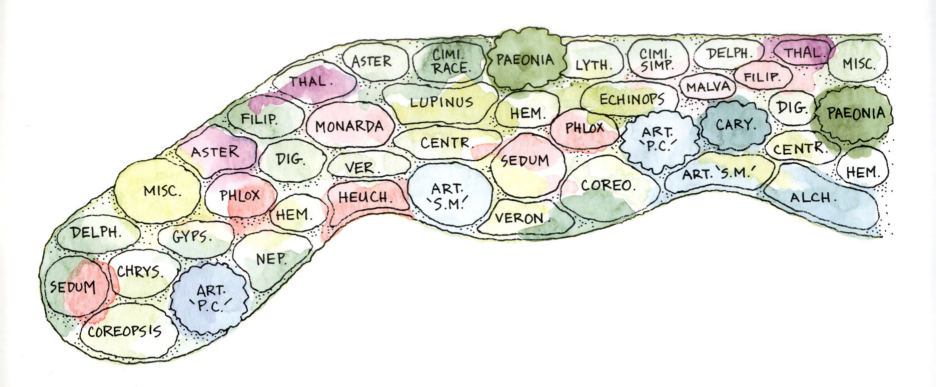

A Border in Northern Westchester
Designed by Lisa Stamm and Dale Booher

Site: Full sun

Soil: Slightly acid loam

Zone: 6b

PLANT LIST

PERENNIALS

Alchemilla mollis *Lady's-mantle*
Artemisia 'Powis Castle'
A. schmidtiana 'Silver Mound'
Aster 'Alma Potschke',
   'Harrington's Pink', and
   'Summer Sunshine'

Astilbe, small pink
Caryopteris
Centranthus ruber
   Red valerian
Chrysanthemum 'Little Princess'
Cimicifuga racemosa
   Snakeroot
C. simplex 'White Pearl'
Coreopsis verticillata
   Tickseed
Delphinium 'Bluebird'
D. elatum 'Pacific' hybrids
Digitalis 'Excelsior' hybrids
   Foxglove
Echinacea purpurea 'Bright Star'
   Coneflower
Echinops ritro
   Small globe thistle

Filipendula rubra 'Venusta'
   Meadowsweet
Gypsophila paniculata 'Bristol
   Fairy' *Baby's-breath*
Hemerocallis 'Annie Welch',
   'Mary Todd', and 'Stella de
   Oro' *Daylily*
Heuchera 'Coral Cloud' *Alumroot*
Iris ensata 'Haku Boton'
   Japanese iris
I. sibirica 'Caesar's Brother'
   Siberian iris
Lupinus 'Russell Strain'
Lythrum virgatum 'Morden Pink'
   Loosestrife
Malva moschata *Musk mallow*
Miscanthus sinensis
   'Gracillimus'

Monarda didyma 'Croftway Pink'
   Bee balm, Oswego tea
Nepeta mussinii *Catmint*
Paeonia var. *Peony*
Pennisetum 'Hamlin'
   Fountain grass
Penstemon
Phlox carolina 'Miss Lingard'
Sedum purpureum 'Autumn Joy'
   Stonecrop
Stachys byzantina (S. lanata)
   Lamb's-ears
Thalictrum rochebrunianum
   Meadow rue
Veronica 'Crater Lake Blue' and
   'Icicle' *Speedwell*

ANNUALS

Nicotiana alata *Flowering tobacco*

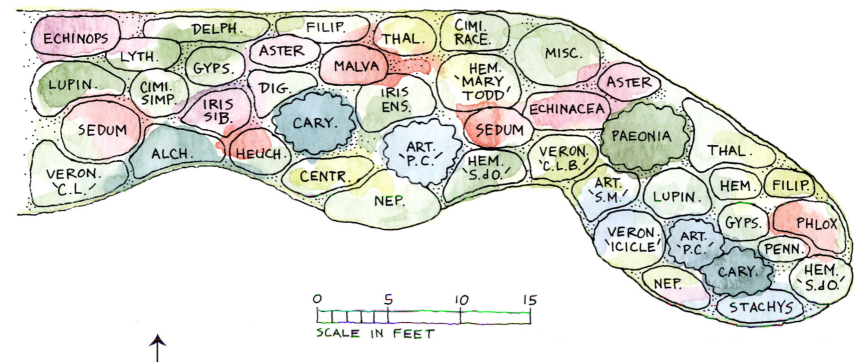

0   5   10   15

SCALE IN FEET

N

Planters filled with ivy,
Salvia, and pink Verbena
punctuate a terrace
overlooking the lawn and
border.

CHAPTER TWELVE

Temperate Oasis

About fifty miles from the great conservatories of the New York Botanical Garden and the Brooklyn Botanic Garden is a house that appears to be much like the others in a neighborhood of small farms, old clapboard houses, and quiet, unpaved roads. Even the trip up the gravel driveway doesn't alert you to what lies beyond, unless you happen to take your cue from the large circular bed of elephant's-ears (Colocasia esculenta) in the middle of the driveway. Behind the house, though, is a garden surrounding a pool that is reminiscent of nothing so much as one of those conservatories filled with the collections of botanists whose passion for exotic plants took them around the world to seek out new and rare specimens.

If the breeze is right, you'll notice the fragrance of this garden long before you actually see it. This is especially so in high summertime, when plants such as Hyssopus, Clethra, Nicotiana, and Monarda fill the air with heavy perfume. But the visual effect is just as intoxicating. Not only are the colors rich and varied, with combinations of orange, scarlet, and lavender a common sight, but everywhere familiar plants are growing in unfamiliar circumstances. Scented Pelargonium grows between Asclepias tuberosa (butterfly weed) and Verbascum, while Cucurbita maxima (Hubbard squash) clambers around clumps of Salvia azurea pitcheri and Miscanthus sinensis 'Variegatus'. And the same Colocasia esculenta that fills a bed in the middle of the driveway is planted so that its huge leaves ripple the surface of the intensely blue pool.

The driving force behind this amazing garden is a woman whose ardor for growing unusual and wonderful plants is tempered only by time, two children, and an equal ardor for unusual and wonderful textiles, which she both collects and

Everything about this garden speaks of the exotic, from the borders surrounding, and often flowing into, the pool, to the faience color of the pool itself and the plant material used, to the strong fragrance that pervades the air.

At the southeastern corner of the pool, Papaver rhoeas, Lythrum, Hemerocallis, and Lilium henryi bloom in front of the foliage of Euphorbia marginata and Colocasia esculenta. OPPOSITE: *Between the pool and the lawn, a group of beds with a red color scheme radiates outward through orange to yellow. Some pinks, such as the Echinacea, and silvers, such as the Artemisia, are remnants of a pastel color scheme.*

creates. To aid her in her determination to make the pool garden unique, in 1986 she recruited artist and landscape designer Hitch Lyman, whose knowledge of plants she sums up as "just incredible. There isn't anything he doesn't know."

The garden has evolved considerably in its four years, each change making color a more dominant feature. In the first year, the borders were pink, pale blue, and yellow. Mr. Lyman, who likes white gardens, was pleased, realizing that his favorite color vanishes in strong light and would be senseless for a poolside garden that gets most of its visitors in the middle of the day. The following year, the two collaborators made the garden predominantly blue. Then the owner wanted to add orange and purple. At that Hitch Lyman was tempted to dig in his heels. But as his misgivings had been proven wrong before, he went along with the owner. "She was," he says, "right again. The faience-blue of that pool kills anything around it except the strongest possible colors."

When our pictures were taken, the group of borders between the lawn and the pool were in transition again. The plan was to put the strong reds in the middle, and fade through orange to yellow at the outer-most fringes. But leftovers from prior stages caused some exciting color combinations, such as the fuchsia-pink of the newcomer Phlox paniculata 'Starfire' with the silvery foliage of Artemisia 'Silver Queen,' a carry-over from the pastel phase.

Mr. Lyman runs through these schematic changes breezily, as though switching the colors of a border amounts to nothing more complex than changing your shirt. Conceptually, to him it probably doesn't. He describes his profession as teaching people how to garden, and although this underplays his many other talents, he is a gifted teacher. His advice tends to be extremely clarifying, with remarks such as "First decide about basic areas of color. Once you have those drawn in, if you see a new plant, you'll know where to plug it in. Also, you will know what you need."

Hitch Lyman also cautions against expecting too long a season of one border. The pool borders, for example, are spectacular from July through September, and even that, he thinks, is asking a lot. Other months are left to other areas around the house, which means that when Mr. Lyman or the owner comes across an irresistible new plant, no matter when it blooms, they won't have to do without it.

LEFT: *Elsewhere around the pool are tucked such striking plants as the tender bulb Tigridia pavonia.* RIGHT: *Tangles of boldly colored annuals, such as red and orange Cosmos, lavender Ageratum, and the blue-and-white Convolvulus tricolor 'Blue Ensign', contribute to the sense of ebullience of this garden.*

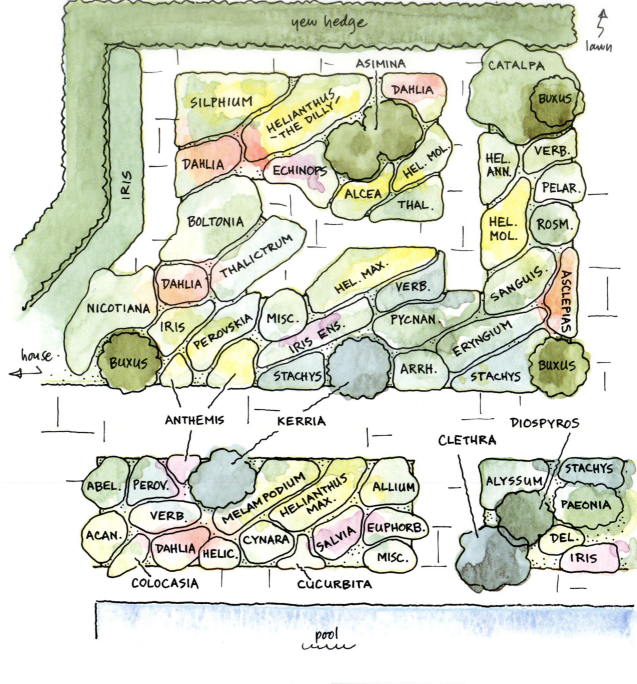

"White Meadows Farm"
Westchester County,
New York
Designed by Hitch Lyman

SITE: Full sun

SOIL: Slightly acid loam

ZONE: 6b

PLANT LIST

PERENNIALS

Alcea rosea *Hollyhock*
Anthemis tinctoria 'E. C. Buxton'
  Golden marguerite
Artemisia 'Silver Queen'
Astilboides tabularis
Boltonia asteroides
Caryopteris
Clematis 'Etoile Rose'
Crambe cordifolia *Colewort*
C. maritima *Sea kale*
Crocus speciosus
Delphinium
Echinacea purpurea
  Coneflower
Echinops ritro and E. r. 'Veitch's
  Blue' *Small globe thistle*
Eryngium amethystinum
Glechoma hederacea variegata
  (Nepeta hederacea)
  Runaway Robin
Helianthus 'Autumn Beauty'
  Sunflower
H. maximiliani
  Maximilian sunflower
H. mollis *Ashy sunflower*
Hemerocallis, pale yellow *Daylily*
Hibiscus 'Diana'
  Rose-of-Sharon
Hosta plantaginea 'Newport Blue'
Inula magnifica
Iris ensata *Japanese iris*
Lilium 'Black Stallion'
L. henryi
L. speciosum 'Album'
Lobelia cardinalis *Cardinal flower*
L. x gerardii
L. siphilitica *Blue cardinal flower*
L. splendens 'Queen Victoria'
Lythrum *Loosestrife*
Miscanthus sinensis 'Morning
  Light'
Melampodium padulosum
Monarda didyma 'Adam' and
  'Cambridge Scarlet'
  Bee balm, Oswego tea

Paeonia 'Black Dragon'
  Peony
Pennisetum alopecuroides
Perovskia atriplicifolia
  Russian sage
Phlox paniculata 'Mt. Fuji' and
  'Starfire' *Garden phlox*
Pycnanthemum muticum
  Mountain mint
Salvia azurea pitcheri

Sanguisorba canadensis
  Canadian burnet
Stachys byzantina (S. lanata)
  Lamb's-ears
Silphium perfoliatum *Cup plant*
Thalictrum dipterocarpum
  Meadow rue

ANNUALS

Abelmoschus 'Mischief'
  Musk mallow
Acanthus balcanicus
  Bear's-breech
Agrostemma nulas *Corn cockle*
Allium christophii and
  A. spaerocephalum
Alyssum maritimum
  (Lobularia maritima)

Antirrhinum *Snapdragon*
Arrhenatherum elatius var.
  bulbosum 'Variegatum'
  Tuber oat grass
Brachycome
Cleome *Spider plant*
Colocasia esculenta
  Elephant's-ear
Cucurbita maxima
  Hubbard squash

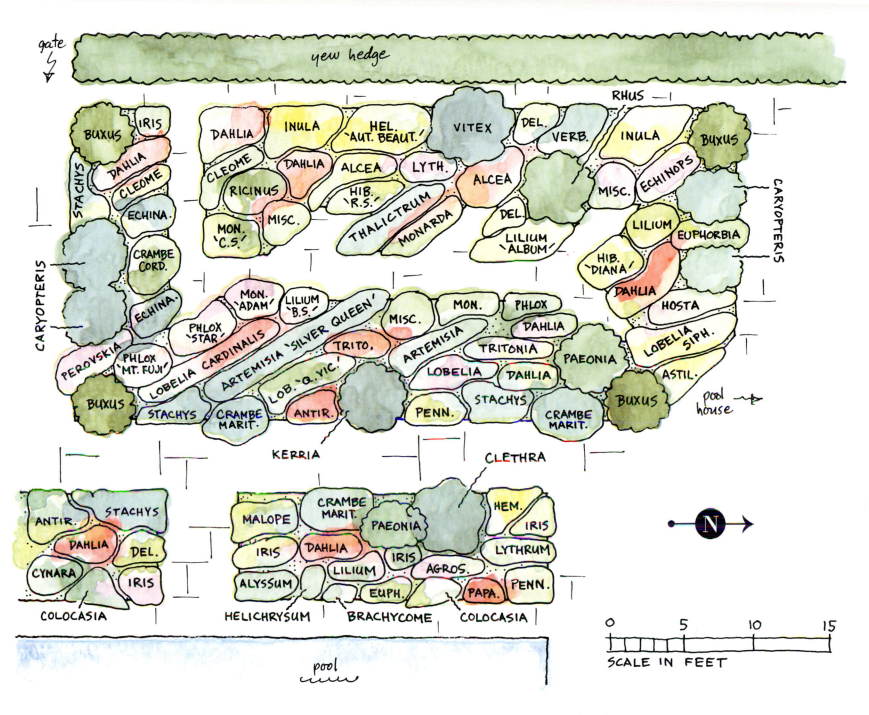

gate

yew hedge

RHUS

BUXUS
IRIS
STACHYS
DAHLIA
CLEOME
ECHINA
CRAMBE CORD.
ECHINA.
PEROVSKIA
BUXUS

CARYOPTERIS

DAHLIA
CLEOME
RICINUS
MON. 'C.S.'
MISC.
INULA
DAHLIA
ALCEA
HIB. 'R.S.'
HEL. 'AUT. BEAUT.'
LYTH.
THALICTRUM
MONARDA
VITEX
ALCEA
DEL.
VERB.
DEL.
LILIUM 'ALBUM'
INULA
MISC.
ECHINOPS
BUXUS
LILIUM
EUPHORBIA
HIB. 'DIANA'
DAHLIA
HOSTA

CARYOPTERIS

PHLOX 'STAR'
MON. 'ADAM'
LILIUM 'B.S.'
PHLOX 'MT. FUJI'
LOBELIA CARDINALIS
ARTEMISIA 'SILVER QUEEN'
TRITO.
LOB. 'Q. VIC'
MISC.
ARTEMISIA
MON.
TRITONIA
LOBELIA
PHLOX
DAHLIA
DAHLIA
PAEONIA
LOBELIA SIPH.
ASTIL.

BUXUS
STACHYS
CRAMBE MARIT.
ANTIR.
PENN.
STACHYS
CRAMBE MARIT.
BUXUS

pool house

KERRIA

CLETHRA

ANTIR.
STACHYS
DAHLIA
DEL.
CYNARA
IRIS
COLOCASIA

MALOPE
CRAMBE MARIT.
IRIS
DAHLIA
PAEONIA
IRIS
LILIUM
AGROS.
ALYSSUM
EUPH.
PAPA.
HEM.
IRIS
LYTHRUM
PENN.

HELICHRYSUM
BRACHYCOME
COLOCASIA

N

pool

0					5		10		15

SCALE IN FEET

Cynara cardunculus *Cardoon*
Dahlia vars.
Emilia javanica (E. flammea)
 Tassel flower,
 Flora's-paintbrush
Euphorbia marginata
 Snow-on-the-mountain
Helianthus annuus 'Italian White'
 Common sunflower

Helichrysum petiolatum
 Licorice plant
Hibiscus 'Red Shield'
Malope trifida
Nicotiana sylvestris
 Flowering tobacco
Papaver rhoeas
 Field or Flanders poppy
Pelargonium *Geranium*

Ricinus 'Carmencita'
 Castor-oil-plant
Rosmarinus *Rosemary*
Tritonia (Montbretia)
Verbascum *Mullein*
Vitex agnus-castus, white
 Indian-spice

Shrubs
Asimina triloba *Pawpaw*
Buxus *Box*
Catalpa
Clethra alnifolia
 Sweet pepperbush
Cotinus coggygria (Rhus
 cotinus) *Smokebush*
Diospyros *Persimmon*
Kerria japonica *Japanese rose*

Three-Part Harmony

It is probably safe to assume that every house that has been preserved as a monument to its era has a story behind it. These houses often embody something much deeper than good architecture; when the passion of the family who built it subsides, a house's longevity is directly allied to how much passion it evokes in others.

In 1894, Augustus Van Wickle bought a thirty-three-acre estate overlooking Narragansett Bay in a town called Bristol, Rhode Island, reputedly because he needed a place to moor his new yacht. The property had a substantial collection of rare trees, and it was to be those trees, and Mr. Van Wickle's additions to them, that were to generate enough passion in his descendants to ensure that the house was preserved.

By the time Marjorie Lyon, the daughter of Augustus Van Wickle, left Blithewold, as the house was named, to the Heritage Foundation of Rhode Island in 1976, the Van Wickle family had seen it through eighty-two years. Their affection for it had endured a fire that destroyed the first house they'd built, the death of Mr. Van Wickle in a hunting accident, and the remarriage of his widow. Mrs. Lyon's will held a little surprise for any who didn't know what part of Blithewold truly held her heart: it stipulated that her endowment be used for the maintenance of the gardens, and only leftover funds for the house.

Blithewold's mixed borders lie in what was once a formal parterre filled with multicolored annuals and crisscrossed with gravel paths. But Marjorie Lyon decided that the design was too labor-intensive and that it competed with a view over the lawns to Narragansett Bay. She reduced the parterre to its current plan of grass edged with flower beds, and established the blue, white, and yellow color scheme. She achieved a comfortable balance between a design so arresting

A color scheme restricted to blue, white, and yellow lends tranquility to the North Garden at Blithewold, a notion devised to keep the garden from competing with views out over Narragansett Bay.

ABOVE: *Potted violas flank the staircase leading from the house into the North Garden.* RIGHT: *Despite its strict color scheme, the garden has a remarkable variety of flowers. Pale-lavender Campanula lactiflora, violet Delphinium 'Pacific Giant' and Iris sibirica, white Phlox maculata, yellow Oenothera, and chartreuse Alchemilla all bloom in early July.*

OPPOSITE: *Ligularia przewalskii grows behind the similar but paler-flowered Thermopsis caroliniana and a clump of Chrysanthemum x superbum.*

that your eye would never progress out to the Bay, and a design that barely causes it to pause. When you stand in the garden or in the house, your gaze sweeps the borders, lingering among yellow lilies or purple-blue delphiniums, and then continues its course out to Narragansett Bay. Then it is drawn irresistibly back to the borders.

Even after she had removed the multicolored beds, Mrs. Lyon maintained a preponderance of annuals in the borders. And though in the last few years the borders have been generally switched over to perennials, a select group of annuals remains. These, notes staff horticulturist Julie Morris, tend to be chosen more the way perennials are generally chosen — by virtue of their plant form, and not, as is often the case with annuals, solely on the basis of their flowers.

As Blithewold is open to the public, the north borders have to look pretty for as long a season as possible. Whereas annuals are good season-stretchers, especially in late August, when fewer perennials are in bloom, the show is really carried by the perennials. It begins in late April with daffodils, but only a few, because their leaves yellow-off over almost a month, and are in the meantime hard to camouflage. Along with the daffodils, and following them, are early perennials such as Phlox divaricata, Trollius europaeus 'Lemon Queen', and the late tulips 'Queen of the Night' and 'Cream Delight'.

With the Nepeta, peonies, and bearded and Siberian irises coming into bloom, the next stage is largely blue and white. By July, the yellow shows more strongly, with lilies, daylilies, and Ligularia przewalskii in full flower. The Alchemilla mollis, which starts blooming with the peonies, begins to look tired and brown by the end of August, when it is cut back hard to remove all its old leaves. It responds, according to Ms. Morris, by throwing out another set of fresh lime-green foliage. The Nepeta also starts to look fatigued by early July, and at that point is carefully deadheaded, so that it produces a second crop of flowers in August.

This sort of maintenance is routine at Blithewold, where volunteers give the borders a thorough deadheading twice a week. They apply fertilizer to the soil, which is slightly acid, in early spring, early July, and the fall. The organic fertilizer they use curtails mishaps such as burnt foliage from overapplication of chemical mixes. Because of the good care the garden gets, and because its proximity to the Bay forestalls the frost, Blithewold's flower season lasts long into fall. On November 8, Aconitum fischeri, Salvia guaranitica, Aster x frikartii, and the Tagetes tenuifolia 'Lulu' were among the flowers still in bloom. The borders looked more than merely respectable, and it is a safe bet that even Marjorie Lyon, who was known to be a perfectionist, would be pleased with the legacy she left behind.

"Blithewold"
The North Garden
Bristol,
Rhode Island

Site: Full sun

Soil: Slightly acid sandy
loam

Zone: 7a

PLANT LIST

PERENNIALS

Achillea 'Moonshine' *Yarrow*
A. ptarmica 'The Pearl'
   Sneezewort
Aconitum fischeri and A. napellus
   Monkshood
Alchemilla mollis *Lady's-mantle*
Amsonia tabernaemontana
Aquilegia chrysantha *Columbine*
A. 'Maxi Star'
Artemisia abrotanum
   Southernwood
A. 'Powis Castle' and 'Silver
   Queen'
Aster 'Eventide' and 'Professor
   Kippenburg'
A. x frikartii
A. spectabilis
Baptisia australis *False indigo*
Brunnera macrophylla
   Siberian bugloss
Campanula carpatica 'Blue Clips'
   Tussock bellflower
C. lactiflora
C. persicifolia *Willow bellflower*
Caryopteris x clandonensis
   'Blue Mist'
Centaurea montana
   Mountain bluet
Chrysanthemum vars. x
   superbum *Shasta daisy*
Clematis recta
Coreopsis verticillata
   'Moonbeam' *Tickseed*
Delphinium 'Blue Fountains',
   'Dwarf Blue Butterfly', and
   'Pacific Giant'
Dicentra spectabilis
   Bleeding-heart
Digitalis grandiflora 'Temple
   Bells' *Foxglove*
D. lutea
Echinops 'Taplow Blue'
   Globe thistle
Eupatorium coelestinum
   Mist flower, Hardy ageratum

Fern spp.
Hemerocallis vars. *Daylily*
Hosta 'Honeybells' and
   variegated
Iris ensata *Japanese iris*
I. x germanica *Bearded iris*
I. sibirica *Siberian iris*
Kirengeshoma palmata
Lavandula 'Hidcote'
   Lavender
Ligularia przewalskii
   Rocket ligularia
Lilium vars.
Linum perenne *Flax*
Lupine vars.
Lysimachia clethroides
   Gooseneck loosestrife
Monarda didyma 'Blue Stocking'
   Bee balm, Oswego tea
Myosotis alpestris
   Forget-me-not
M. sylvatica *Garden forget-me-not*
Nepeta mussinii *Catmint*
Oenothera tetragona
   Evening primrose
Paeonia 'Prairie Moon' *Peony*
Penstemon barbatus 'Alba'
   Beard-tongue
Perovskia atriplicifolia
   Russian sage
Phlomis russeliana *Jerusalem sage*
Phlox carolina 'Miss Lingard'
P. divaricata *Wild sweet William*
P. paniculata 'Mt. Fujiyama'
   Garden phlox
Platycodon grandiflorus
   Balloon flower
Potentilla warrenii *Cinquefoil*
Rhazya orientalis
Salvia argentea *Silver sage*
S. azurea var. grandiflora
   (S. pitcheri)
S. officinalis 'Tricolor'
S. x superba 'East Friesland'
Stachys byzantina (S. lanata)
   'Silver Carpet' *Lamb's-ears*
S. officinalis *Betony*
Stokesia laevis *Stokes' aster*
Teucrium fruticans *Germander*
Thalictrum aquilegifolium
   Meadow rue
Thermopsis caroliniana
   Carolina lupine
Trollius europaeus 'Lemon
   Queen' *Globeflower*
Veronica 'Blue Charm', 'Crater
   Lake Blue', and 'Shirley Blue'
   Speedwell

ANNUALS

Ageratum 'Blue Horizon'
Asperula orientalis *Woodruff*
Chrysanthemum 'Primrose Gem'
Convolvulus tricolor 'Blue Ensign'
   Dwarf morning-glory
Dahlia 'Irene Van Der Zwet'
Heliotrope
Hibiscus 'Golden Bowl'
Hunnemannia *Mexican poppy*
Lobelia 'Cambridge Blue'
Osteospermum fruticosum
   African daisy
Salvia guaranitica
S. sclarea *Clary sage*
Tagetes tenuifolia 'Lulu'
   Marigold

SHRUBS AND VINES

Hedera helix
Hydrangea macrophylla
Hydrangea anamola petiolaris

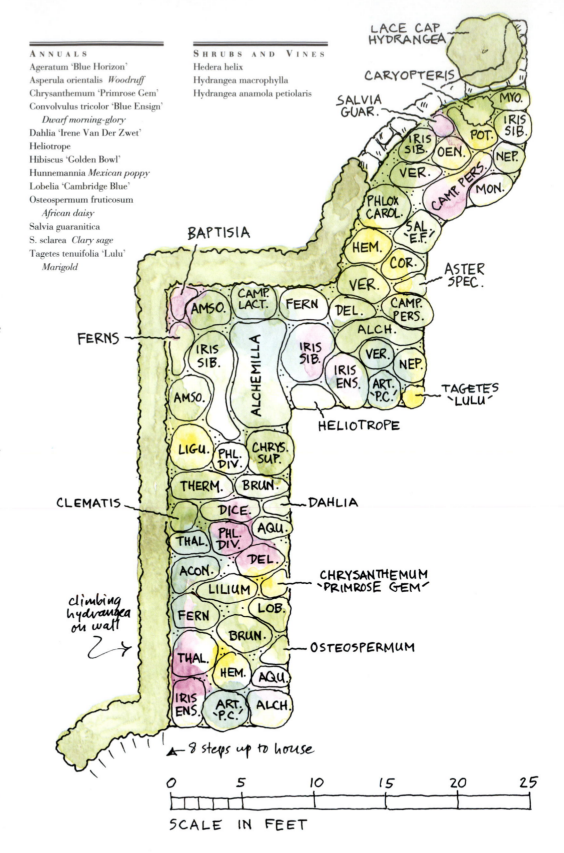

LACE CAP HYDRANGEA
CARYOPTERIS
SALVIA GUAR.
BAPTISIA
FERNS
CLEMATIS
climbing hydrangea on wall
ASTER SPEC.
TAGETES 'LULU'
HELIOTROPE
DAHLIA
CHRYSANTHEMUM 'PRIMROSE GEM'
OSTEOSPERMUM
8 steps up to house

0   5   10   15   20   25
SCALE IN FEET

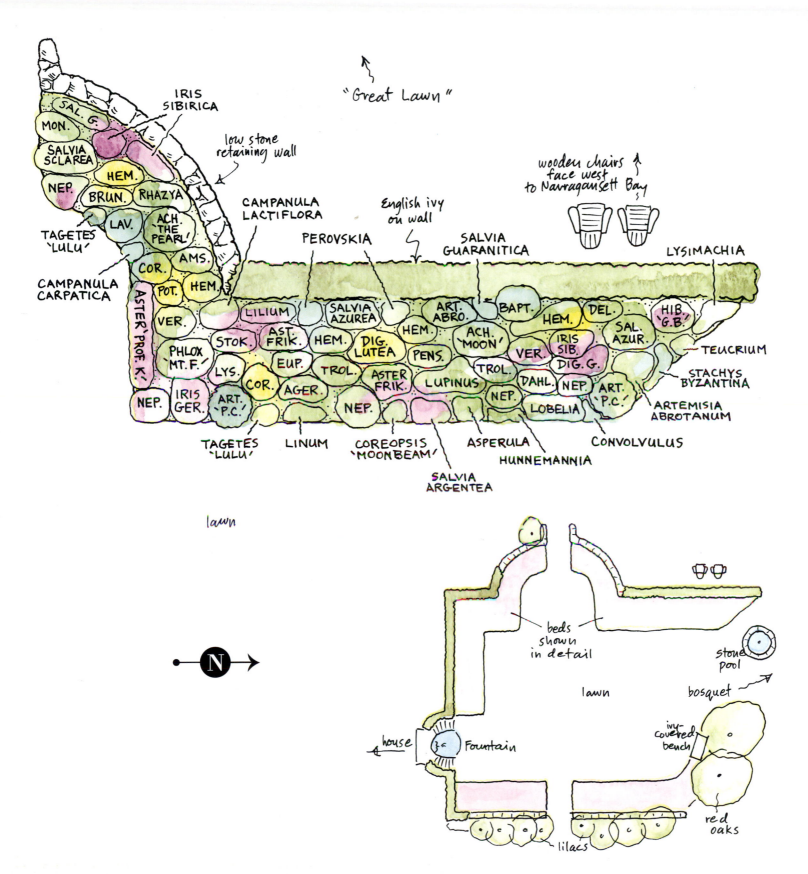

"Great Lawn"

IRIS SIBIRICA

low stone retaining wall

wooden chairs & face west to Narragansett Bay

SAL. G.

MON.

SALVIA SCLAREA

NEP.

HEM.

BRUN. RHAZYA

ACH. 'THE PEARL'

LAV.

CAMPANULA LACTIFLORA

English ivy on wall

SALVIA GUARANITICA

LYSIMACHIA

TAGETES 'LULU'

AMS.

COR.

PEROVSKIA

CAMPANULA CARPATICA

POT. HEM.

VER.

LILIUM

SALVIA AZUREA

ART. ABRO.

BAPT.

HEM.

DEL.

HIB. 'G.B.'

ASTER 'PROF. K.'

STOK.

AST. FRIK.

HEM.

DIG. LUTEA

HEM.

ACH. 'MOON'

SAL. AZUR.

PHLOX MT. F.

EUP.

PENS.

VER.

IRIS SIB.

TEUCRIUM

LYS.

TROL.

ASTER FRIK.

TROL.

DIG. G.

STACHYS BYZANTINA

NEP.

IRIS GER.

COR.

AGER.

LUPINUS

DAHL.

NEP.

ART. 'P.C.'

ART. 'P.C.'

NEP.

NEP.

LOBELIA

ARTEMISIA ABROTANUM

TAGETES 'LULU'

LINUM

COREOPSIS 'MOONBEAM'

ASPERULA

HUNNEMANNIA

CONVOLVULUS

SALVIA ARGENTEA

lawn

N →

beds shown in detail

stone pool

lawn

bosquet

house

Fountain

ivy-covered bench

red oaks

lilacs

Coloring Lessons

Frank Cabot dreams of turning the twenty-odd acres of his garden, which is called Stonecrop, into a school of practical horticulture; although he speaks of this as a goal, in a sense he has already achieved it. For more than thirty years he has grown an ever-widening variety of plants, establishing what will, and what won't, thrive on his windy hilltop site, and he shares his hard-won information with the public by allowing them to visit (by appointment) and to buy plants. In 1986, Mr. Cabot employed Caroline Burgess, an English horticulturist who had trained at the Royal Botanic Gardens at Kew, and the flow of new plants and knowledge into Stonecrop became a flood.

In the enclosed flower garden, Ms. Burgess experiments not just with horticulture but with color, turning the area into what might be called a border-design laboratory. Having inherited the diagonal pattern of square borders, she took out most of the existing vegetables, cutting flowers, and roses, and established a color scheme for the garden. Orbiting around a central square of gray is an array of beds in a loosely followed rainbow, from white and pastel colors, clockwise to red, orange, and yellow, then to green, blue, and violet. At the opposite end of the garden, past the cutting and vegetable beds, are six beds arranged in an even stricter rainbow. These, instead of being broken down into specific colors, fade gradually from one hue to the next: an even more exacting science.

Experience leads Ms. Burgess to be a great proponent not only of plants that are rare in cultivation but of some remarkably common ones; to her, the criterion is not how rare a plant is but how well it suits her needs. Hence her borders have some plants that aren't listed in *Hortus Third*, the horticultural authority, such as

The walled garden in mid-July. On the right, Filipendula ulmaria spills onto the path from the White bed. Opposite it, in the Old Rose bed, is the pale pink Papaver nudicaule 'Cedric Morris'.

Plectostachys serpyfolia, a gray-leaved white everlasting, and Chrysanthemopsis hosmariense, a ten-inch mound-forming plant with daisylike flowers. But the borders also contain impatiens, begonias, and chrysanthemums — plants she once found pedestrian but is now happy to have.

Ms. Burgess advises all gardeners to concentrate on what they can grow. As Delphinium, for example, despises the heat and humidity of her locale, she suggests Campanula, Adenophora, Salvia, Buddleia, and a non-hardy shrub that she grows as an annual (with the aid of a greenhouse) called Oxypetalum caeruleum as substitutions. Salvia, in fact, is something of a specialty at Stonecrop, where more than sixty annual and perennial varieties of the genus are grown. They provide flowers in blue, yellow, pink, white, lavender, salmon, and red, plus large, felted leaves (S. argentea) and variegated leaves and purple leaves (S. officinalis 'Tricolor' and 'Purpurea'), and they come in a range of heights. For American gardeners, they are an undiscovered goldmine.

Caroline Burgess also recommends annuals, biennials, and plants such as snapdragons (Antirrhinum)

that are actually tropical perennials but can be brought to flower swiftly enough to be treated as annuals. Some that grow in the flower-garden borders are Papaver nudicaule, Verbena bonariensis, the biennial Onopordum, and the purple-leaved basillike Perilla frutescens 'Crispa'. The latter three self-seed in the garden, an added bonus. Annual climbers such as sweet peas, Cobaea scandens, Tropaeolum (nasturtium), and Eccremocarpus scaber scramble up the tripods, and bring Stonecrop's total count to well over two hundred varieties of annuals.

With a boost from this huge assortment of annuals, Ms. Burgess keeps the show going in the flower borders from April until October — no small feat, even in a garden this extensive. Yet, amazingly, Caroline Burgess establishes her color schemes for a border and then goes immediately to planting: she maps her garden based on how she planted it, not the reverse. She finds this method easier, but it has to be remembered that she is a consummate plantswoman who has a nursery full of both rare and common annuals and perennials to facilitate her task, and a talent for selecting them.

"Stonecrop"
Garden of
Frank Cabot
Cold Spring,
New York
Designed by
Caroline Burgess

SITE: Sunny, protected by board fence

SOIL: Clay, improved with manure

ZONE: 6a

PLANT LIST

WHITE BED

PERENNIALS

Ajuga *Bugleweed*
Allium cowanii
A. pulchellum album
Artemisia camphorata
Aster, white
A. novi-belgii 'Snowsprite'
Bellis perennis 'Alba'
   English daisy
Bergenia
Boltonia asteroides
Campanula trachelium
   'Album'
   Nettle-leaved bellflower
Carex *Sedge*
Chrysanthemopsis hosmariense
Chrysanthemum frutescens
   'White Pompon'
C. serotinum (C. uliginosum)
   Giant daisy
C., white
Cimicifuga japonica var. acerina
C. racemosa
Cynara cardunculus
   Cardoon
Delphinium, white
Dianthus 'Aqua' and
   'Mrs. Sinkins'
D. barbatus 'Alba'
Dicentra spectabilis 'Alba'
   Bleeding-heart

Digitalis purpurea 'Alba'
   Foxglove
Echinacea purpurea 'White
   Lustre' *Coneflower*
Epimedium niveum
Filipendula ulmaria
   Queen-of-the-meadow
Foeniculum vulgare *Fennel*
Geranium, white
G. phaeum album
Gypsophila paniculata 'Bristol
   Fairy' *Baby's-breath*
Hesperis matronalis 'Alba'
   Dame's rocket
Heuchera *Alumroot, Coralbells*
Hosta, variegated
Iris x germanica, white
   Bearded iris
Lamium 'White Nancy'
   Dead nettle
Lavatera 'Mont Blanc'
   Tree mallow
Leucojum aestivum (bulb)
   Giant snowflake
Liatris pycnostachya 'Alba'
Lilium 'Juliana'
Limonium sinuatum 'Alba'
Lunaria annua variegata *Honesty*
Lychnis chalcedonica 'Alba'
   Maltese cross
Lysimachia clethroides
   Yellow loosestrife, Circle flower
Malva moschata 'Alba'
   Musk mallow
Mentha x rotundifolia variegata
Miscanthus sinensis 'Gracillimus'
Monarda 'Snow White'
   Bee balm, Oswego tea
Myrrhis odorata
   Myrrh, Sweet cicely
Narcissus 'February Silver'
Nepeta 'Snowflake' *Catmint*
Pachysandra terminalis
Paeonia lactiflora *Garden peony*

Phalaris arundinacea 'Picta'
   Canary grass
Phlox divaricata 'Fuller's White'
   Wild sweet William
Physostegia virginiana 'Summer
   Snow' *Obedient plant*
Plectostachys serpyfolia
Polemonium caeruleum 'Alba'
   Jacob's-ladder
Reseda alba *Mignonette*
Rosa 'Ilse Krohn' (against fence),
   'Pax', 'White Dawn' (climbing
   up fence), and white
Rumex scutatus 'Silver Lining'
   French sorrel
Salvia
S. verticillata 'Alba'
S. viridis (S. horminum),
   rose/peach
Sanguisorba obtusa
   Japanese burnet
Scabiosa caucasica 'Alba'
Silene 'Robin Whitebreast'
   Catchfly
Stokesia laevis 'Silver Moon'
   Stokes' aster
Thymus 'Silver Queen'
Viola cornuta 'White Perfection'
   Horned violet

ANNUALS

Acidanthera (tender corm)
   Peacock orchid
Antirrhinum 'White Wonder'
   Snapdragon
Argyranthemum foeniculacium
Cosmos 'Purity'
Gladiolus 'St. Mary'
   (tender corm)

Moluccella laevis *Bells-of-Ireland*
Nicotiana longiflora
N. sylvestris
Nigella damascena, white
   Love-in-a-mist
Petroselinum crispum 'Afro'
   Parsley
Plectranthus coleoides
   Swedish begonia
Viola x wittrockiana 'Floral
   White' *Pansy*

VINES

Clematis henryi
C. lanuginosa 'Candida'
C. paniculata
Hydrangea anomala subsp.
   petiolaris (up peach tree)
Wisteria sinensis 'Alba'

SHRUBS

Chaenomeles nivalis (espaliered
   on fence) *Flowering quince*
Euonymus 'Variegata'
Pieris

TREES

Peach

*Hemerocallis 'Mary Anne'
and Achillea 'Salmon
Beauty' represent two
of the most reliable
perennial clans for
midsummer blooms.*

Stonecrop's Enclosed Garden

[garden diagram labels: white bed; white, pink, & pastel square; gray square; tool house; vegetables; garden room]

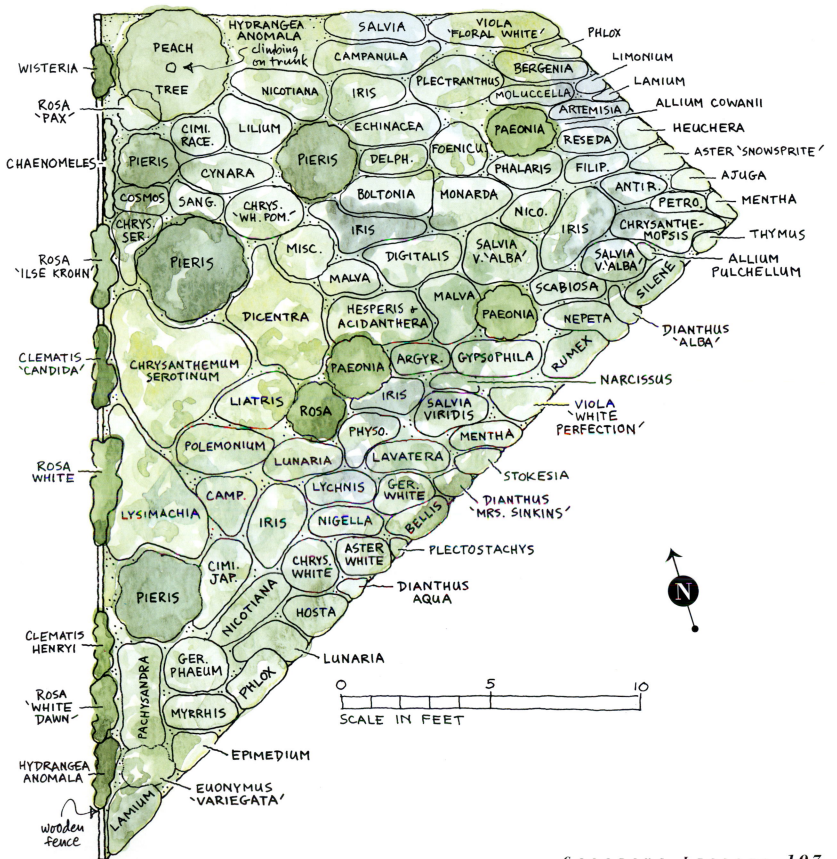

WISTERIA

ROSA 'PAX'

CHAENOMELES

ROSA 'ILSE KROHN'

CLEMATIS 'CANDIDA'

ROSA WHITE

CLEMATIS HENRYI

ROSA 'WHITE DAWN'

HYDRANGEA ANOMALA

wooden fence

PEACH TREE

HYDRANGEA ANOMALA climbing on trunk

SALVIA

VIOLA 'FLORAL WHITE'

PHLOX

LIMONIUM

LAMIUM

ALLIUM COWANII

HEUCHERA

ASTER 'SNOWSPRITE'

AJUGA

MENTHA

THYMUS

ALLIUM PULCHELLUM

DIANTHUS 'ALBA'

NARCISSUS

VIOLA 'WHITE PERFECTION'

STOKESIA

DIANTHUS 'MRS. SINKINS'

PLECTOSTACHYS

DIANTHUS AQUA

LUNARIA

EPIMEDIUM

EUONYMUS 'VARIEGATA'

CAMPANULA

NICOTIANA

IRIS

PLECTRANTHUS

BERGENIA

MOLUCCELLA

ARTEMISIA

PAEONIA

RESEDA

CIMI. RACE.

LILIUM

ECHINACEA

FOENICU.

PHALARIS

FILIP.

ANTIR.

PETRO.

PIERIS

CYNARA

PIERIS

DELPH.

CHRYSANTHE-MOPSIS

COSMOS

SANG.

CHRYS. 'WH. POM.'

BOLTONIA

MONARDA

NICO.

IRIS

CHRYS. SER.

MISC.

IRIS

DIGITALIS

SALVIA V. 'ALBA'

SALVIA V. 'ALBA'

SILENE

PIERIS

MALVA

MALVA

SCABIOSA

DICENTRA

HESPERIS & ACIDANTHERA

PAEONIA

NEPETA

CHRYSANTHEMUM SEROTINUM

PAEONIA

ARGYR.

GYPSOPHILA

RUMEX

LIATRIS

ROSA

IRIS

SALVIA VIRIDIS

POLEMONIUM

PHYSO.

MENTHA

LUNARIA

LAVATERA

CAMP.

LYCHNIS

GER. WHITE

BELLIS

LYSIMACHIA

IRIS

NIGELLA

CIMI. JAP.

CHRYS. WHITE

ASTER WHITE

NICOTIANA

HOSTA

PIERIS

GER. PHAEUM

PHLOX

LUNARIA

PACHYSANDRA

MYRRHIS

LAMIUM

SCALE IN FEET

0   5   10

N

PERENNIALS

Achillea 'Salmon Beauty' *Yarrow*
Allium schoenoprasum 'Forsgate'
Anthemis tinctoria 'Wargrave'
   Golden marguerite
Artemisia ludoviciana 'Valerie
   Finnis'
Aster 'Snowball' and violet
A. tradescantii
Baptisia leucantha
   White false indigo
Bergenia
   'Bressingham White'
Boltonia asteroides 'Pink Beauty'
   and 'Snowbank'
Campanula persicifolia
   Willow bellflower
C. punctata rubrifolia
Chelone glabra
   Turtlehead

Coreopsis rosea
   Tickseed
Delphinium tatsienense
   'Alba'
Dianthus barbatus, pink and white
D. spp., compact pink
Dicentra 'Zestful'
   Bleeding-heart
Dictamnus albus *Gas plant*
Gaura lindheimeri
Geranium endressii *Cranesbill*
G. pratense, pink
Gypsophila oldhamiana
G. paniculata 'Pink Star'
   Baby's-breath
Hemerocallis 'Mary Anne' *Daylily*
Iris x germanica, white
   Bearded iris
I. pallida 'Dalmatica'
Kniphofia 'White Fairy'
   Red-hot poker
Lavandula angustifolia 'Nana'
   Lavender
Lavatera thuringiaca 'Barnsley'
   Tree mallow
Limonium sinuatum, light blue
   Statice, Sea lavender

Malva moschata 'Alba'
   Musk mallow
Marrubium velvetissimum
   Horehound
Monarda didyma 'Croftway Pink'
   Bee balm, Oswego tea
Paeonia, white *Peony*
Phlox carolina 'Miss Lingard'
P. paniculata 'Dodo Hans-
   bury Forbes'
   Garden phlox

Platycodon, blue
   Balloon flower
Polemonium
   caeruleum 'Alba'
   Jacob's-ladder
Polygonum 'Border Jewel'
   Knotweed
Sanguisorba obtusa *Burnet*
Sedum spectabile *Stonecrop*
Stachys betonica 'Rosea'
   (S. officinalis)
Tradescantia 'Pauline' *Spiderwort*
Viola cornuta 'White Perfection'
   Horned violet
V. 'Maggie Mott'

Ageratum 'Bavaria' *Flossflower*
Antirrhinum 'Rocket Pink' and
   white with purple eye
   Snapdragon
Argyranthemum foeniculacium
   A. 'Mary Wootten'
     Chrysanthemum
      Starburst hybrids

Cleome '
   Helen Campbell'
   Spider plant
Consolida 'Pink Perfection'
   Larkspur
Diascia *Twinspur*
Fuchsia 'Little Jewel'
F. microphylla
Heliotropium arborescens 'Alba'
   Heliotrope
Hypoestes 'Pink Splash'
Lychnis coeli-rosa 'Cardinalis'
   Rose-of-heaven
L. coronaria auculiata, white
   Rose Campion
Matthiola, pink *Stock*

Nicotiana 'Daylight'
   Flowering tobacco
Nierembergia, white *Cupflower*
Salvia greggii, white *Autumn sage*
S. involucrata *Rosy-leaf sage*
S. 'Pink Sunday'
S. sclarea var. turkestaniana
   Clary
S. viridis (S. horminum),
   rose/peach
Senecio vira-vira
Silybum marianum *Holy thistle*
Verbena 'Silver Anne' and white
   Vervain
Viola, wild variety, self seeded
Zinnia 'Peter Pan', white

Clematis macropetala
   'Markham's Pink'
C. montana 'Marjorie'
C. virginiana
Cobaea scandens 'Alba'
   Cup-and-saucer vine
Lathyrus 'Lillie Langtry'
   Annual sweet pea
L., pink
Rosa 'Pompom de Paris' and
   'Swan Lake'

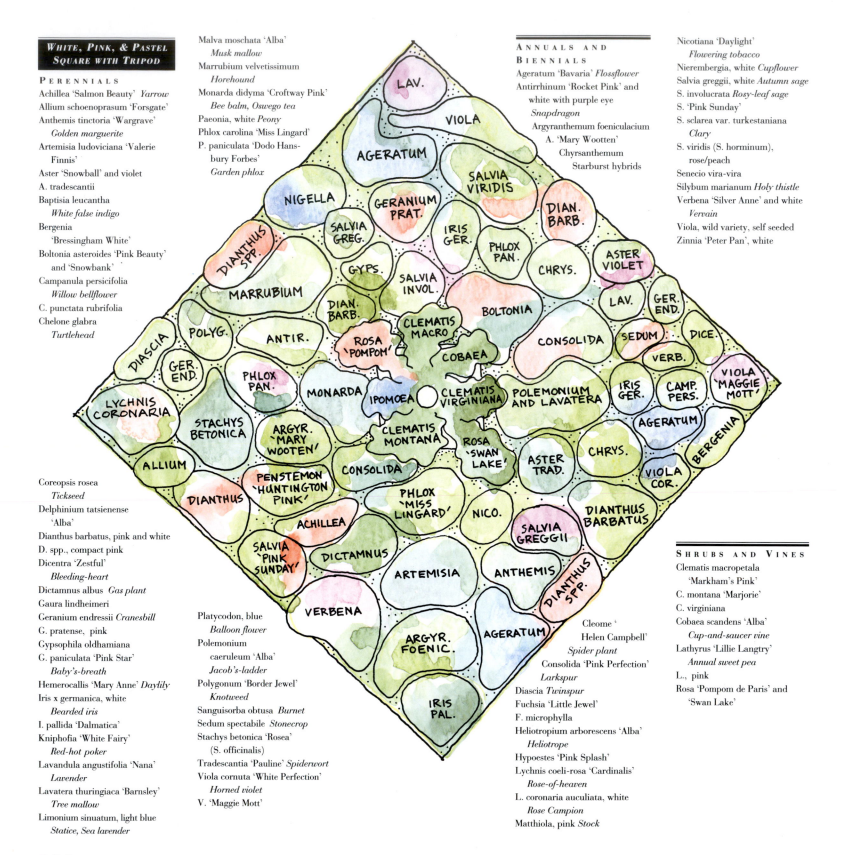

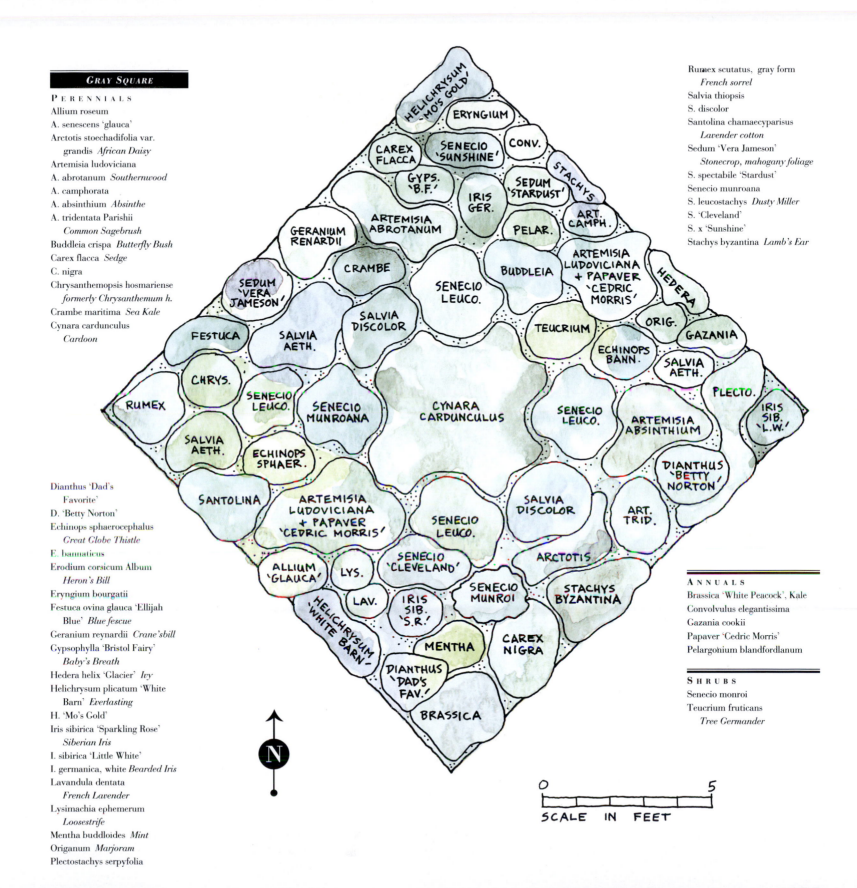

Big Splash

You don't often see gardeners taking out huge sections of ancient privet hedge so that an already ample lawn can sweep into the one adjoining it. In fact, gardeners generally try to tame enormous spaces by making them into "rooms," with hedges, fences, walls, and arbors. That's because most people are more comfortable in smaller gardens, with their controlled views and sense of intimacy. But Tish Rehill, who with her husband, Michael Doherty, designed this border, wasn't worried about the scale of the space she was creating. She knew, however, that ripping out the privet and combining several small borders into one 225-foot-long carpet of flowers would create problems of a different sort, both horticultural and aesthetic.

For starters, the condemned privet hedge

The view northward along the border, from a blue, pink, and white section with Nepeta, Stachys, and the cream- and green-leaved Phalaris to a yellow-and-orange section of plantings.

blocked not just a vista (the motivation for its removal) but a strong wind from the ocean. She would have to make her design gale-proof. Furthermore, the immense border would be visible not only from the house but from a path that runs along it. So it would have to be successful both from a distance, competing with all that wide-open space for attention, and on an intimate level.

Ms. Rehill might have responded to such a sizable border by filling it with enormous single-variety drifts. Instead, she divided the border into seven sections, each about twenty-five feet wide. Starting at each end are yellow-orange sections; pink, white, and blue sections; then the yellow and red sections that Ms. Rehill calls the "Mexican" color groups; and finally, at the center, a deep-purple and bronze section. Viewed from a distance, each color group has the same dynamism that a single plant has at closer range. In both cases, you can appreciate the variations of color, texture, and form.

Ms. Rehill filled each area with a complex

selection of plants in groups of three, five, or, occasionally, as few as one. Although any one section could stand alone in a smaller garden as its own border, Ms. Rehill wove them together, using related or similar plants in adjacent sections. A Lysimachia punctata in the yellow-orange sections, for example, is emulated by Lysimachia clethroides in the pink, white, and blue sections. Similarly, the soft mounded form of Santolina in the yellow-orange group is picked up by Nepeta in the pink-white-blue group, and continued with Lantana in the Mexican group. It's a very subtle repetition, and it keeps the border cohesive.

Tish Rehill knew when she opened up the privet hedge that she would have to allow the forces of wind and weather to help select her plant material. Peonies, Cimicifuga (snakeroot), Delphinium, and Digitalis purpurea were among the first casualties to the constant salt spray. But some plants seem to revel in the coastal weather. The Grecian foxglove, Digitalis lanata, holds up well, as does the August-blooming blue-purple Lobelia x gerardii (also called L. x vedraiensis). Aconitum henryi 'Spark's Variety', with deep violet-blue flowers in late July and early August, is a surprising success, and the Santolina and lavenders thrive in the warm, sandy soil. Another plant that appreciates conditions in the border is the fragrant purple Verbena bonariensis, whose three- to four-foot wiry stems need no staking, even in this windy spot, and whose spent flowers drop off, so it never requires deadheading.

Part of the joy of this garden, for an inveterate tinkerer like Ms. Rehill, is finding new plants and color combinations. She lists "oddball annuals" in the border as some of her favorites. The Mexican bush sage, Salvia leucantha, began blooming in June, and was still flowering in early November. Another sage, the purple-leafed Salvia officinalis purpurascens, and an edible grain called orach (Atriplex hortensis 'Rubra'), which has strong red foliage, thrive in the central purple-red section of the border. The Lantana adds potent color to the border, especially in the hot-pink and orange range. The border also has clumps of scented geraniums (Pelargonium), some of which have beauti-

OPPOSITE: *A view from the southern end of the border in June shows in the foreground the grasslike Acorus, yellow Lysimachia, orange Geum, and yellow-leaved Spiraea 'Goldflame'.* ABOVE: *A view from the Mexican section toward the pool garden. In the purple section are Allium giganteum and the leafy dark-purple stalks of Atriplex hortensis.* LEFT: *Large, oblong drifts running parallel to the border ensure that faded plants are soon obscured by the growth of plants around them. The Stachys and Nepeta, seen here in June, will be sheared back in July. By late summer the blooms of Aster frikartii (here just a clump of green foliage on the left) will fountain over the Nepeta.*

Ms. Rehill mixes the warm coppery reds of the purple-leaf sand cherry (Prunus x cistena) with the acid yellow and lime green of Alchemilla and Angelica. Woven through the middle are the warmer yellow and orange of Lysimachia and Geum. Seen on their own, the yellow-orange sections of the border create a bit of tension—which is relieved as the eye travels along the rainbow of colors in the rest of the border.

ful flowers in addition to their attractive foliage. Ms. Rehill often lifts these in the fall, trimming them into a nice ball and bringing them indoors in pots for the winter.

Knowing that room can always be found for new plants is only one of the advantages of a border this varied and large. The owners, and Ms. Rehill, can also afford to be relaxed about cutting flowers — for obvious reasons taboo in a smaller garden. Ms. Rehill is known to wander through the tall grasses at the back of the border, collecting bucketfuls of Allium, Verbena, and anything else that strikes her. As she points out, "On an average day, there are probably more than seven hundred plants in bloom in the border. That's a lot of flowers."

That many flowers means a lot of maintenance. The border requires constant weeding, fertilizing, deadheading, and removal of old or dead plants. Surprisingly, though, it is not watered. A few feet below the surface, the soil is hard clay. Ms. Rehill discovered that water couldn't penetrate the clay, so it accumulated above it and caused some plants to rot. Believing that soil "is what the plants live in, so getting it right only makes sense," she first added sand to help the water dissipate, and continues to dig in leaf mold yearly as a conditioner.

Most gardens are constantly evolving, and this one is no exception. Given owners who are enthusiastic gardeners and who love to bring home new ideas from their travels, coupled with Ms. Rehill's own propensity for additions and changes, the garden could never become static. Each season brings new combinations, new colors, and new design variations. The northern end of the border, which once petered out in a thin strip of pale orange and yellow flowers against a huge, unclipped section of privet, has been redesigned so that the border will now end in a strong, and much wider, flourish of purple and yellow. The next planned change is a spring display of masses of Iris reticulata, crocuses, and parrot- and lily-flowered tulips, all organized within the color boundaries of the border.

As the yellow-orange section flows into its pink-white-blue neighbor, Ms. Rehill replaces the coppery reds and oranges with pink and purple tones. Here, yellow Lysimachia and Centaurea (the yellow thistlelike flower in the foreground) contrast with rosy-pink Liatris and purple-pink Lythrum.

*Garden in Eastern
Long Island,
New York
Designed by
Tish Rehill and
Michael Doherty*

SITE: Sunny

SOIL: Shallow loam over clay

ZONE: 7a

PLANT LIST

YELLOW-ORANGE

PERENNIALS

Achillea 'Coronation Gold'
Yarrow

Acorus gramineus variegatus
'Ogon' (Carex variegata)
Grassy-leaved sweet flag

Alchemilla mollis
Lady's-mantle

Centaurea macrocephala

Crocosmia 'Lucifer'

Echinacea purpurea 'Bright Star'
Coneflower

Gaillardia x grandiflora 'Tokajer'
Blanket flower

Geum quellyon 'Mrs. Bradshaw'

Helenium autumnale *Sneezeweed*

Helianthus salicifolius

Iris pseudacorus *Yellow iris*

Kniphofia uvaria *Red-hot poker*

Liatris spicata *Gay-feather*

Lobelia cardinalis
Cardinal flower

Lysimachia punctata
Yellow loosestrife, Circle flower

Lythrum virgatum 'Dropmore
Purple' *Loosestrife*

Monarda didyma 'Cambridge
Scarlet' and 'Violet Queen'
Bee balm, Oswego tea

Panicum virgatum 'Rehbraun'
Switch-grass

Pennisetum alopecuroides

Santolina virens

Sedum purpureum 'Autumn Joy'
Stonecrop

Verbascum olympicum *Mullein*

ANNUALS

Angelica archangelica
Wild parsnip

Cleome 'Violet Queen'

Lantana

SHRUBS

Buddleia davidii 'Royal Red'
Butterfly bush

Prunus x cistena

Spiraea x bumalda 'Goldflame'
Bridal-wreath

PINK, WHITE & BLUE

PERENNIALS

Aconitum henryi 'Sparks
Variety' *Monkshood*

Artemisia ludoviciana
'Silver King'

Aster x frikartii 'Monch'

Aster novi-belgii 'Snow Flurry'

Baptisia australis *False indigo*

Chrysanthemum x superbum
'May Queen' and
'Thomas E. Killen' *Daisy*

Coreopsis verticillata 'Moonbeam'
Tickseed

Echinacea purpurea 'Bright Star'
Coneflower

Eryngium amethystinum

Geranium endressii 'Wargrave
Pink' *Cranesbill*

Iris ensata 'Haku Botan'
Japanese iris

I. siberica 'Caesar's Brother' and
'Dewful' *Siberian iris*

Liatris spicata 'Alba'
Gay-feather

Lobelia x gerardii

Lysimachia clethroides
Gooseneck loosestrife

Malva alcea var. fastigiata

Nepeta x faassenii 'Six Hills
Giant' *Catmint*

Perovskia atriplicifolia
Russian sage

Phalaris arundinacea 'Picta'
Canary grass

Salvia sclarea var. turkestaniana

Sanguisorba canadensis
Canadian burnet

S. obtusa *Japanese burnet*

Santolina virens

Saponaria officinalis 'Flore Plena'
Bouncing Bet

Sedum purpureum 'Autumn Joy'
Stonecrop

Sidalcea malviflora *Checkerbloom*

Stachys byzantina (S. lanata)
Lamb's-ears

Veronicastrum virginicum
Bowman's-root

ANNUALS

Agrostemma githago 'Milas'
Corn cockle

Antirrhinum, pink *Snapdragon*

Cleome 'White Queen'

Salvia farinacea 'Indigo Spires'

S. leucantha *Mexican bush sage*

BULBS

Acidanthera murieliae
Peacock orchid

Galtonia candicans
Summer hyacinth

Lilium henryi

Polianthes tuberosa, single *Tuberose*

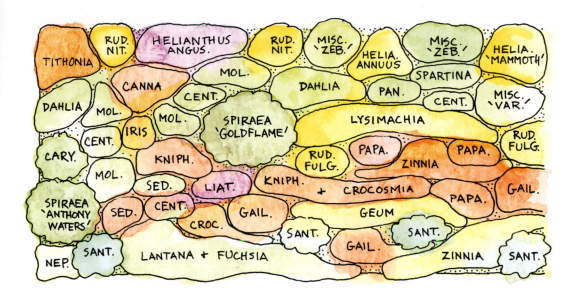

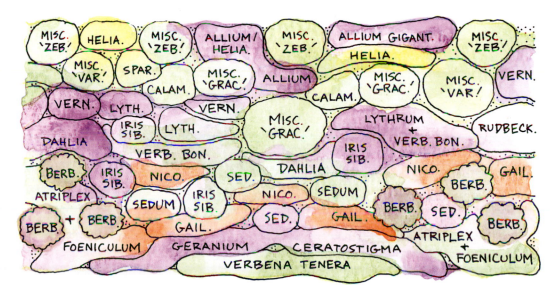

N

PURPLE

PERENNIALS

Anchusa azurea 'Lodden Royalist'
  Bugloss, Alkanet
Calamagrostis acutaflora stricta
Ceratostigma plumbaginoides
  Plumbago
Gaillardia x grandiflora
  'Burgundy'
  Blanket flower
Geranium 'Johnson's Blue'
  Cranesbill
Iris ensata 'Nikko' *Japanese iris*
I. siberica 'Caesar's Brother'
  Siberian iris
Lavandula
Lobelia x gerardii (Lobelia
  vedraiensis)
Lythrum virgatum 'Dropmore
  Purple' *Loosestrife*
Miscanthus sinensis 'Gracillimus'
  and 'Variegatus'
M. sinensis 'Zebrinus'
  Zebra grass
Salvia officinalis purpurascens
Sedum purpureum 'Autumn Joy'
  Stonecrop
Spartina pectinata 'Aureo-
  marginata' *Prairie cordgrass*
Vernonia noveboracensis
  Ironweed

ANNUALS

Atriplex hortensis 'Rubra'
  Orach, Mountain spinach
Foeniculum vulgare 'Bronze'
  Fennel
Helianthus annuus 'Italian White'
  and 'Luna'
Heliotropium 'Marine'
Nicotiana alata 'Scarlet'
Verbena bonariensis *Vervain*
V. tenera

SHRUBS

Berberis thunbergii 'Crimson
  Pygmy' *Barberry*

MEXICAN

PERENNIALS

Centaurea macrocephala
Crocosmia 'Lucifer'
Digitalis lanata *Grecian foxglove*
Gaillardia x grandiflora 'Tokajer'
  Blanket flower
Geum quellyon 'Lady Strathden'
Helianthus angustifolius
  Swamp sunflower
Iris pseudacorus *Yellow iris*
Kniphofia uvaria 'Goldmine',
  'Primrose Beauty', and
  'Vanilla'
Liatris spicata *Gay-feather*

Lysimachia punctata
  Yellow loosestrife, Circle flower
Miscanthus sinensis 'Variegatus'
M. sinensis 'Zebrinus'
  Zebra grass
Molina caerulea arundinacea
  'Skyracer' *Moor grass*
Nepeta x faassenii 'Six Hills
  Giant' *Catmint*
Panicum virgatum
  Switch-grass
Papaver orientale 'Brilliant'
  Oriental poppy
Rudbeckia fulgida 'Goldsturm'
  Black-eyed Susan

R. nitida 'Autumn Glory'
Santolina virens
Sedum purpureum 'Autumn Joy'
  Stonecrop
Spartina pectinata 'Aureo-
  marginata' *Prairie cordgrass*

ANNUALS

Antirrhinum 'Black Prince'
  Snapdragon
Fuchsia
Helianthus annuus 'Italian White',
  'Luna', and 'Mammoth'
  Common sunflower

Lantana 'Confetti'
Tithonia 'Torch'
  Mexican sunflower
Zinnia angustifolia and orange sp.

SHRUBS

Caryopteris x clandonensis
  'Longwood'
Spiraea x bumalda 'Anthony
  Waters' and 'Goldflame'
  Bridal-wreath

0   5   10   15
SCALE IN FEET

BIG SPLASH 117

The Complete Plantswoman

Lynden Miller once told me that she doesn't care nearly as much about a plant's flowers as she does about its form and foliage. "Since most perennials bloom for only two weeks," she says, "why are we so fixated on their flowers?" But on a chilly May day in 1990, Mrs. Miller, a professional landscape designer, surveyed her border, which was a lush tapestry of greens and silvers and coppery reds, and implored, "Bloom, please!"

Of course, it did. In fact, every year it blooms in such profusion that you would never suspect that its owner thinks flowers are of secondary importance. In the spring, her peonies, drooping with huge pink and white blooms, leave you agog. They are joined by reddish pink Centranthus ruber, and the purple-blue of an Iris sibirica and Nepeta x faassenii. Later in the summer, her

The gate by the driveway offers a view of the Miller garden that scarcely hints of the size and complexity of the borders beyond.

garden produces a second spectacle of flowers with plants such as the aptly named Phlox paniculata 'Bright Eyes', the crimson powderpuffs of the annual Gomphrena, and a lemon-yellow Hemerocallis of unknown name. Though all enrapture her, she sees them as icing on the cake, and no amount of icing, in her mind, can save a bad cake.

As a result, a lot of the sparkle in her border comes from plants that are not in flower. This isn't something you pick up on immediately: most people assume that so much color comes from flowers. A sweeping gaze around the borders in late July takes in clumps of pink, lavender, purple, cream, chartreuse, silvery blue, and yellow. The pink, lavender, and yellow come from flowers. But the purple is from Berberis and Cotinus foliage, and the cream and silvery blue come from grasses such as Miscanthus and Helictotrichora, and from the foliage of plants such as Artemisia and Perovskia. Chartreuse is contributed by the broccolilike flower heads of Sedum,

Although July brings the pink flowers of Phlox 'Bright Eyes', much of the border's color comes from foliage. Plants such as Berberis 'Rosy Glo' and 'Crimson Pygmy' form mounds of wine-red, Artemisia and Helictotrichon are silvery blue, and Sedums, still in bud, are a pale bluish green.

still in tight bud and suggesting not even a drop of their future scarlet color.

A painter before she was a gardener, Mrs. Miller understands that the picture you see from afar often differs from what you see close up, and that, in a garden as in art, both should be beautiful. Her border, soft and almost misty from a distance, offers vignettes that only become apparent at about five feet. From far away, mounds of silver, green, and blue, which are the bolder forms, and in this case often just foliage, dominate, but closer inspection reveals blossoms such as the dark-blue annual Salvia farinacea 'Victoria', mauve Thalictrum, or a spray of the silvery-pink Salvia sclarea var. turkestaniana.

Creating this sort of intrigue doesn't come easily. Watching Lynden Miller in her border might give you

acute neurosis unless you understand why she zooms around the place like some supercharged bumblebee. Like most perfectionists, she has too much on her agenda to sit, or stand, still. While she discourses about gardening, she weeds, or snips, or stares with consternation at some plant, wondering how to improve a composition. She isn't one to wait around for the right time to move a plant, either. When the new arrangement occurs to her, chances are she'll create it quickly — maybe even within minutes.

Mrs. Miller's border is testimony to ten years of that kind of concentration, but there is another spot, tucked behind the back of the border, where she does the real experimenting. Ideas that occur in the car, or in the middle of the night, or standing in the border, often get a test run here. While her border is always on view, this little enclosure is strictly off-stage, which means she can be more daring.

One day Mrs. Miller was in the nursery, as this little garden is called, when she passed a yellow-leaved barberry growing beside a shrub with deep maroon leaves. The combination was like a scream. It wasn't just the colors that made her recoil; it was the fact that both were on compact shrubs, so they looked like bright blobs of paint. The colors themselves, she pointed out, could work together given the right textural combination, though she wouldn't isolate a mix like that lemon yellow and reddish purple in an otherwise mellow scheme. (Overall, she noted, the barberry would do better beside a blue-green grass.)

The nursery also serves as a place to test whether plants have the stuff to survive in northwestern Connecticut. Here she checks new plants, which she continually seeks out, assessing not just whether they'll prosper but how best to handle them. "I put in a group of one plant variety, and then I cut one plant down and leave one up. I mulch one, and leave another bare. Then I see what I've got the following spring."

In just about every Miller-designed garden, there will be one or two tall, silvery gray plants called Scotch thistle, or Onopordum acanthium. These are among her favorite plants, and thanks to all her experimentation, she knows that she can prolong their season into late July by punctiliously removing the plant's small pink flowers as they fade. As a result, she enjoys Scotch thistle from peony time in the spring until the beginning of phlox season, at which point she allows the plant to set seed, and then cuts it to the ground. It is a biennial, so those seeds will produce a plant the next spring that will flower the following year.

Mrs. Miller's enthusiasm for plants with strong sculptural form is well known. Henry Fuller weeds and mows lawns for Mrs. Miller, and because it's the kind of job where one quick cut or pull could undo years of work, he is probably one of her most trusted aides. Recently he announced that he had left standing a group of burdock, a huge, vigorous weed, because he wasn't sure whether Mrs. Miller admired the plant. Anywhere

else, that remark might have seemed bizarre — burdock is the kind of weed that most gardeners despair of eliminating — but Mr. Fuller knew what he was talking about. The plant has huge velvety leaves, dark brown beneath and bright green above, on a tall, rough stalk. It is safe to assume that if Mrs. Miller had any hope of controlling it, there would be some burdock in her border.

In early June, the silvery form of the biennial Onopordum acanthium rises between a white peony and a blue Siberian iris.

In the border west of the rose arbor, a lablab bean (Dolichos lablab) grows up an etagere. Behind the Phlox, Cimicifuga and Miscanthus sinesis 'Variegatus' add cream and green to the composition. The lacy silvery foliage is Perovskia on the left and Artemisia 'Silver King' on the right.

OPPOSITE: *Looking west from the middle of the eastern-most border in late July. In the foreground are maroon Berberis 'Crimson Pygmy', the silvery-blue of the grass Helichtotrichon, and the purple-pink flower-heads of the Sedum 'Vera Jameson'. The tall creamy-leafed plant in the center is Salvia sclarea var. turkestaniana, in front of it is dark blue S. 'Victoria', and the rosy flowers on tall wiry stems to its left are Verbena banariensis.*

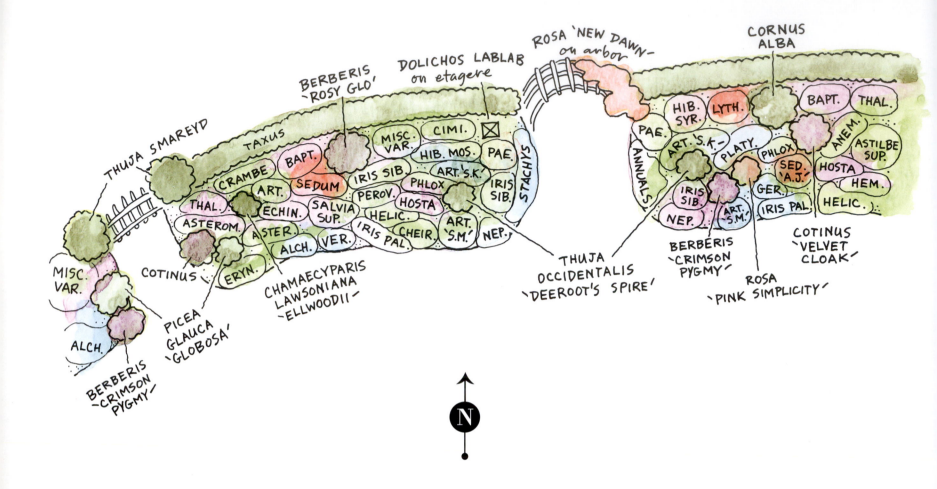

Labels on the garden map:

CORNUS ALBA

ROSA 'NEW DAWN' on arbor

DOLICHOS LABLAB on etagere

BERBERIS 'ROSY GLO'

THUJA SMAREYD

TAXUS

HIB. SYR.   LYTH.   BAPT.   THAL.

PAE.   ANNUALS   ART. 'S.K.'   PLATY.   PHLOX   ANEM.   ASTILBE SUP.

MISC. VAR.   CIMI.   ⊠   SED. A.J.   HOSTA   HEM.

HIB. MOS.   PAE.   IRIS SIB   GER.   HELIC.

CRAMBE   BAPT.   IRIS SIB   ART. 'S.K.'   STACHYS   NEP.   ART. 'S.M.'   IRIS PAL.

SEDUM   PHLOX   IRIS SIB.

THAL.   ART.   PEROV.   HOSTA

ASTEROM.   ECHIN.   SALVIA SUP.   HELIC.   ART. 'S.M.'   NEP.

ASTER   CHEIR.

COTINUS   ALCH.   VER.   IRIS PAL.

MISC. VAR.   ERYN.

ALCH.

BERBERIS 'CRIMSON PYGMY'

PICEA GLAUCA 'GLOBOSA'

CHAMAECYPARIS LAWSONIANA 'ELLWOODII'

THUJA OCCIDENTALIS 'DEEROOT'S SPIRE'

BERBERIS 'CRIMSON PYGMY'

ROSA 'PINK SIMPLICITY'

COTINUS 'VELVET CLOAK'

N

Garden of Lynden B. Miller Northwestern Connecticut

SITE: Sunny

SOIL: Slightly acid loam

ZONE: 5b

PLANT LIST

PERENNIALS

Alchemilla mollis *Lady's-mantle*
Allium tomentosum
Anemone japonica 'September Charm' *Japanese anemone*
Artemisia 'Powis Castle'
A. ludoviciana 'Silver King'
A. schmidtiana 'Silver Mound'
Aster x frikartii
Asteromoea mongolica
Astilbe x arendsii 'Deutschland'
A. taquetti 'Superba'
Baptisia australis *False indigo*
Centranthus ruber *Red valerian*
Cheiranthus 'Bowles Mauve' *Wallflower*
Cimicifuga racemosa *Snakeroot*
Clematis 'Ramona'
Crambe cordifolia *Colewort*
Dianthus
Echinacea purpurea *Coneflower*
Eryngium giganteum
Geranium 'Johnson's Blue' *Cranesbill*

Helictotrichon *Blue oat grass*
Helleborus
Hemerocallis, yellow *Daylily*
Hibiscus moscheutos *Swamp rose mallow*
H. syriacus 'Blue Bird' *Rose-of-Sharon*
Hosta 'Royal Standard' and unnamed spp.
H. sieboldiana 'Frances Williams'
H. sieboldii
Iris laevigata 'Variegata'
I. pallida 'Variegata' *Orris*
I. siberica *Siberian iris*
Lobelia siphilitica *Blue cardinal flower*
Lythrum virgatum 'Morden Pink' *Loosestrife*
Miscanthus sinensis 'Gracillimus'
M. sinensis 'Variegatus'

Nepeta x faassenii *Catmint*
Paeonia vars., pink and white *Peony*
Perovskia atriplicifolia *Russian sage*
Phalaris *Canary grass*
Phlox paniculata 'Bright Eyes' *Garden phlox*
Platycodon *Balloon flower*
Salvia x superba 'East Friesland'
S. turkestaniana
Sedum purpureum 'Autumn Joy' *Stonecrop*
S. 'Ruby Glo' and 'Vera Jameson'
Stachys
Thalictrum 'Lavender Mist' *Meadow rue*
Veronica 'Sunny Border Blue' *Speedwell*

ANNUALS AND BIENNIALS

Dolichos lablab *Hyacinth bean*
Gomphrena 'Lavender Lady' *Globe amaranth*
Heliotrope 'Marine'
Nicotiana langsdorfii
Onopordum acanthium *Scotch thistle*
Salvia farinacea 'Victoria' *Mealy-cup sage*
Verbena bonariensis *Vervain*

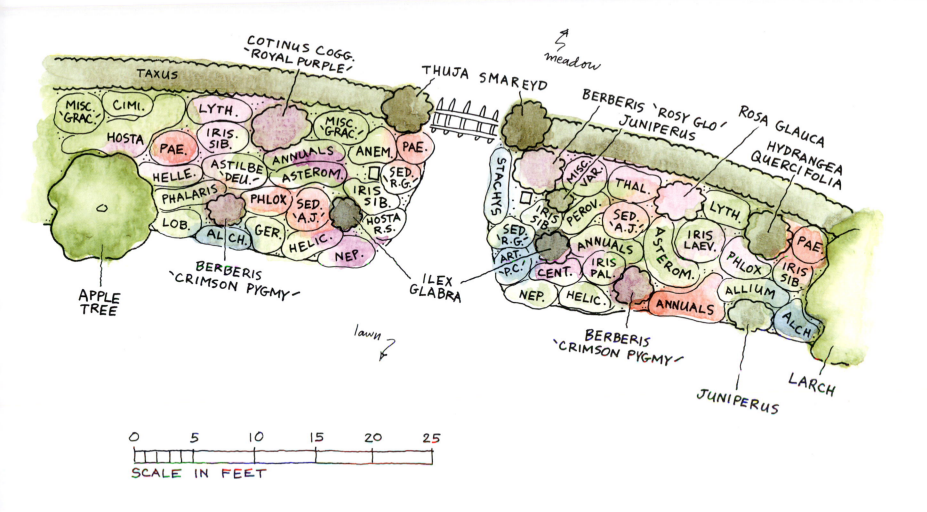

COTINUS COGG. 'ROYAL PURPLE'

THUJA SMAREYD

meadow

BERBERIS 'ROSY GLO' JUNIPERUS

ROSA GLAUCA

HYDRANGEA QUERCIFOLIA

TAXUS

MISC. 'GRAC.' CIMI. LYTH. MISC. 'GRAC.' PAE.

HOSTA IRIS SIB. ANNUALS ANEM.

PAE. ASTILBE 'DEU.' ASTEROM. SED. R.G.

HELLE. PHLOX IRIS SIB.

PHALARIS SED. 'A.J.' HOSTA R.S.

LOB. ALCH. GER. HELIC.

NEP.

STACHYS MISC. VAR. THAL.

SED. R.G. IRIS SIB. PEROV. SED. 'A.J.' LYTH.

ART. P.C. ANNUALS ASTEROM. IRIS LAEV. PHLOX PAE.

CENT. IRIS PAL. IRIS SIB.

NEP. HELIC. ANNUALS ALLIUM ALCH.

APPLE TREE

BERBERIS 'CRIMSON PYGMY'

ILEX GLABRA

lawn

BERBERIS 'CRIMSON PYGMY'

JUNIPERUS

LARCH

0   5   10   15   20   25

SCALE IN FEET

Shrubs

Berberis 'Crimson Pygmy' and 'Rosy Glo' *Barberry*

Chamaecyparis lawsoniana 'Ellwoodii' *False cypress*

Cornus alba 'Elegantissima' *Tartarian dogwood*

Cotinus coggygria 'Royal Purple'

C. 'Velvet Cloak' *Smokebush*

Hydrangea quercifolia *Oak-leaf hydrangea*

Ilex glabra *Winterberry*

Juniperus squamata 'Blue Star'

Paeonia suffruticosa *Tree peony*

Picea glauca globosa *White spruce*

Rosa glauca

R. 'New Dawn' and 'Pink Simplicity'

Thuja *Arborvitae*

T. occidentalis 'Deeroot's Spire' *American arborvitae, White cedar*

T. smareyd 'Emerald Green'

Taxus x media 'Hicksii' *Yew*

The flowering of the peonies marks the start of the main season in this and many another border.

The Quintessential Flower Garden

In early April, the scene inside the walled garden at Old Westbury is one of relative serenity. Three gardeners are at work, planting pansies and weeding. There is a lot of freshly turned earth in evidence, and the bright green of new growth, but few flowers. By the end of April, though, when the gardens open to the public, that will have changed. Five thousand tulips will have begun to unfurl, launching a spectacle that continues with annuals and perennials throughout the summer, and whose finale is the flowering of dahlias and chrysanthemums in the fall.

By the time the gardens close in early November, the greenhouse staff will have already started cuttings for the following year's show. Lists will be completed for the reordering of seeds, and the fall-blooming plants will be pulled out and replaced with tulip bulbs. All winter long, more than four thousand annual seedlings will get a jump on life in the greenhouses, and in March, dahlias will be potted up and kept indoors, so that they will bloom in July, a full month earlier than if they were planted outside after the last frost. In April, it will all begin again, completing a cycle that has continued, almost unchanged, since the English architect George Crawley designed the New York house and gardens for financier John S. Phipps and his wife in 1906.

Old Westbury is gardening on a grand scale. And though one might think that if there had been any changes over the years they would have been to scale things down, it seems to have been the opposite. The house was not generally used by the Phipps family during the summer, so emphasis in the borders was on spring and fall. But when Mr. Phipps died in 1958, the property was bought by the J. S. Phipps Foundation, and it is now open to the public from late April until early November. Because the borders at Old West-

At Old Westbury, the focus is on flowers, producing a breathtaking, albeit high-maintenance, result. This is bed Y in late July.

bury comprise what is emphatically a *flower* garden, the effort required to keep it in a state of permanent abundance is monumental. Perennials such as Anchusa, delphiniums, Campanula, and poppies, which in other gardens are permanent fixtures, are pulled out immediately after they bloom in early June. They are replaced with later-blooming annuals such as zinnias, cleomes, salvias, and snapdragons, many of which in turn are replaced by chrysanthemums in early September.

There is logic in this. The plants in the 88-by-160-foot walled garden are chosen for their flowers. Almost without exception, they are beautiful in bloom but look dull, if not abysmal, when their flowers start to fade. Pointedly omitted are plants whose form and foliage make them pretty all season long, but whose flowers aren't spectacular: ornamental grasses, lady's-mantle, and (except in deeply shaded corners) hostas, or any of the dwarf evergreens or non-flowering deciduous shrubs such as barberry. In most gardens, foliage plants not only carry the border over from one flower-burst to the next, they also provide a sense of architecture. At Old Westbury, architecture comes from brick walls with pilasters, gateways capped with carved limestone, and reflecting pools and fountains. The plantings scarcely need to add to it.

Kim Johnson is the walled-garden supervisor, which means she does everything from weeding and answering visitors' questions about fertilizer (she does use it — any 5-10-5, applied according to the manufacturer's instructions) to giving lectures on the garden. But her real job is orchestration: deciding what plants to use in the garden and making sure they are purchased, grown, planted, and removed on schedule, and ensuring that all are immaculately maintained year-round. Between Ms. Johnson and the four gardeners who work with her, there are some 20,000 plants to cajole into good behavior.

Central to Ms. Johnson's job are plans that were drawn up in 1959 by Tallahassee landscape architect Barbara Capen. The plans show the walled garden's twenty-eight beds, separated into eight color groups.

Using the plans as a reference point, Kim Johnson has devised work lists for each color group. These specify plants and delineate where and when to place them in the borders, from setting out pansies in early spring and lifting tulips and replanting with summer-blooming plants, to removing faded plants in late summer and planting chrysanthemums. With the work sheets, which are posted in her office, Ms. Johnson organizes the day-to-day tasks of her staff.

Of course, nothing about a garden is ever as predictable as the phrase "day-to-day" suggests. Apart from plants that Kim Johnson expects to replace each year, there are older perennials that need to be either divided into smaller, more vigorous clumps or replaced with new stock. There are plants she wants to test for possible future use as the garden continues to evolve. And there are filler plants such as cleomes, zinnias, and marigolds that are grown in a field behind the walled garden and used as needed.

Old Westbury falls officially into the colder range of hardiness zone 7, but Ms. Johnson has found that the garden sits in a frost pocket, and will get a frost even when gardens a mile away are still frost-free. And, although it is generally said that walled gardens shelter tender species from extreme winter temperatures, Ms. Johnson has found it to be true only in the case of plants actually growing on the walls. There is a Bull bay magnolia (M. grandiflora), for example, on the north wall (facing south), and although the species is marginally hardy in zone 7, it does very well, given the protection of a burlap wrapping for the winter. For the rest, she thinks the wall may actually make life a little tougher on the plants, because the bricks and the bluestone paths tend to hold heat like an oven. So while her plants get little extra warmth in the winter, they are almost literally fried in midsummer.

In 1989, Ms. Johnson embarked on a plan to renovate the borders. Many were weed-infested, and some plants had grown too large. The irises were being consumed by iris borers, and other maladies such as bacterial leaf spot were weakening them further. Beginning in the fall, she and her staff pulled everything out

Although the walled garden has plenty of architectural elements that play against the softness of masses of flowers, many of the borders themselves have neither architectural ornament nor boldly sculptural plants. Instead, some are anchored by stands of strongly colored flowers.

Here, in a July view looking southward along bed E, bright-red snapdragons and zinnias add zest to what would otherwise be a bland scheme.

Bright-pink petunias and sheared Nepeta are used as edging; in the back are pink cleomes.

of beds AA and BB. Into the nursery area went plants that were free of weeds, or could be made that way, and plants that were young and vigorous. All others were discarded. With the beds empty, the staff briefly discussed double-digging the soil (the back-breaking process that gives you rich topsoil about two feet deep), but that idea was vetoed. Knowing that there were twenty-six huge beds still remaining, Ms. Johnson pointed out, would tend to limit anyone's enthusiasm for double-digging.

So the borders were loaded with leaf mulch and rototilled, and in the spring they were rototilled again. Tulips that had been potted up and overwintered in a cooler were set out in early spring, and in May, as the tulips faded, the perennials that had been growing in the nursery beds were replaced in the borders. Most perennials love this treatment; these were no exception, responding so well that the rejuvenated beds were instantly as full and lush as their neighbors, if not more so. Come fall, Kim Johnson and her staff will begin on the next of the borders slated for overhaul, a job that should be completed just in time for spring of 1996, Old Westbury Gardens' ninetieth year.

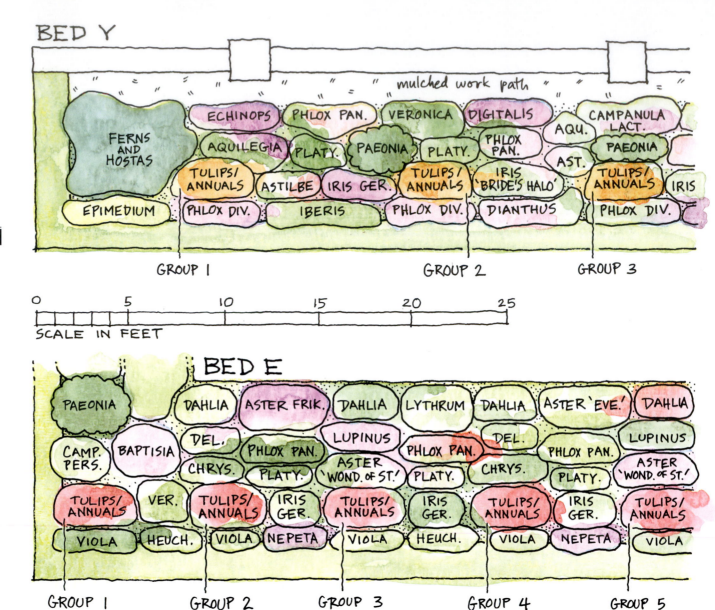

Walled Garden at Old Westbury Gardens
Old Westbury, New York

SITE: Protected, full sun
SOIL: Slightly acid loam
ZONE: 7b

PLANT LIST

BED Y

PERENNIALS

Aquilegia x hybrida 'McKana Giants' *Columbine*

Astilbe x arendsii 'Ostrich Plume'

Campanula lactiflora

C. persicifolia *Willow bellflower*

Chrysanthemum x superbum *Shasta daisy*

Dianthus barbatus 'Newport Pink' *Sweet William* (treated as an annual)

Digitalis purpurea *Foxglove*

Echinops

Epimedium

Iberis sempervirens *Candytuft*

Iris x germanica 'Bride's Halo' (yellow gold) and 'Dark Side' (dark blue) *Bearded iris*

Monarda didyma, lavender-pink *Bee balm, Oswego tea*

Paeonia lactiflora 'Bobby Ann' *Garden peony*

Phlox divaricata 'Fuller's White' *Wild sweet William*

Phlox paniculata, salmon and white *Garden phlox*

Platycodon, blue *Balloon flower*

Thalictrum speciosissimum (T. glaucum) *Meadow rue*

Veronica longifolia *Speedwell*

Plus various Ferns and Hostas at shaded end of border

ANNUALS

Catharanthus roseus 'Blanche' *Madagascar periwinkle*

Chrysanthemum x morifolium 'Crackerjack' (to replace Lantana), 'Red Headliner', and 'Nutmegger' (to replace Catharanthus)

Cleome, white

Cosmos 'Purity'

Dahlia 'Golden Bouquet'

Gaillardia x grandiflora 'Burgundy' *Blanket flower*

Lantana, light yellow

Petunia x hybrida 'Arctic Pearls'

Salvia farinacea, tall light salmon (to replace Digitalis) *Mealy-cup sage*

Tibouchina (grown into bushes; to replace Digitalis and Campanula)

Torenia fournieri 'Compacta Blue' (to replace Dianthus) *Wishbone flower*

Viola x Wittrockiana, white *Pansy*

BULBS

Tulips

PLANTING INSTRUCTIONS

IN EARLY JUNE:

Replace tulips in Groups 1, 3, and 5 with twelve white Catharanthus or white petunias.

Replace tulips in Groups 2, 4, and 6 with two Dahlia.

Replace tulips in Group 7 with Lantana.

IN EARLY JULY:

Replace Digitalis with Salvia and Tibouchina.

Plant Salvia in front of Campanula persicifolia, and Tibouchina in front of C. lactiflora.

Replace Dianthus with Torenia.

IN EARLY SEPTEMBER:

Replace Lantana with Chrysanthemum 'Crackerjack' and Catharanthus with C. 'Nutmegger'. Fill in any holes with C. 'Red Headliner'.

BED E

PERENNIALS

Aster 'Eventide' and 'Harrington's Pink'

A. x frikartii and A. x frikartii 'Wonder of Staffa'

Baptisia australis *False indigo*

Campanula persicifolia *Willow bellflower*

Chrysanthemum parthenium (Matricaria) *Feverfew*

Delphinium

Heuchera

Iris x germanica 'Ballerina', 'Beverly Sills' (pink), 'Black Hills', 'Black Taffeta', 'Bright Cloud', 'Cloud Clap', 'Royal Velvet', 'Spring Festival', lavender and white, and small white *Bearded iris*

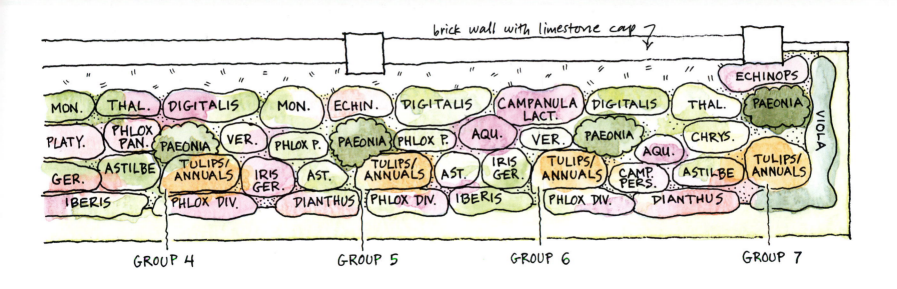

GROUP 4   GROUP 5   GROUP 6   GROUP 7

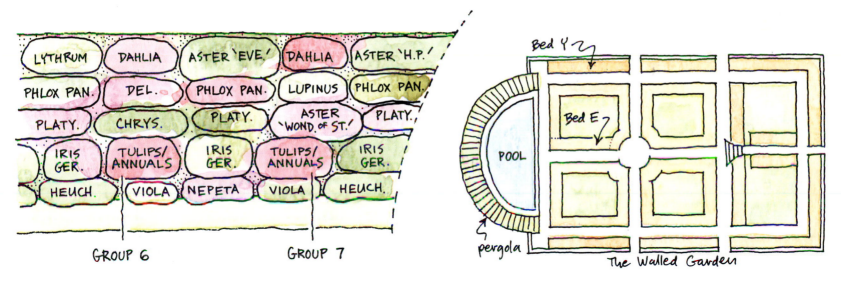

GROUP 6   GROUP 7

The Walled Garden

Lupinus
Lythrum virgatum 'Morden Pink' *Loosestrife*
Nepeta mussinii 'Blue Wonder' *Catmint*
Paeonia suffruticosa *Tree peony*
Phlox paniculata, lavender, light pink, and white *Garden phlox*
Platycodon *Balloon flower*
Veronica longifolia *Speedwell*

ANNUALS
Antirrhinum 'Frontier Crimson' and 'Frontier Red' *Snapdragon*

Ageratum 'Blue Danube'
Catharanthus roseus 'Cooler Peppermint' and 'Little Bright Eyes' *Madagascar periwinkle*
Chrysanthemum x morifolium 'Cloud Nine' (to replace Catharanthus 'Little Bright Eyes'), 'Quaker' (to replace Verbena), 'Pink Daisy' (to replace Ageratum), 'Ruby Mound' (to replace Antirrhinum 'Frontier Red'), and 'Prom Queen' (to fill in holes in border)
Dahlia 'Pink Bouquet'
Petunia x hybrida 'Fallon Blush Pink'

Salvia farinacea 'Blue Bedder' (in front of Delphinium) and 'Victoria' (to fill in) *Mealy-cup sage*
Verbena 'Pink Delight'
Viola x Wittrockiana 'Blue Dream' and white *Pansy*
Zinnia elegans 'Zenith Wild Cherry' (to fill in)

PLANTING INSTRUCTIONS
IN EARLY JUNE:
Replace tulips in Group 1 with Catharanthus 'Little Bright Eyes'.

Replace tulips in Groups 2 and 6 with twelve Antirrhinum 'Frontier Red' and nine Petunia.
Replace tulips in Groups 3, 5, and 7 with two Dahlia and seven Ageratum.
Replace tulips in Group 4 with twelve Antirrhinum 'Frontier Red' and nine Verbena.
IN EARLY JULY:
Plant seven Salvia 'Blue Bedder' in front of each group of Delphinium, and fill holes in the border with Zinnia and Salvia 'Victoria'.

IN EARLY SEPTEMBER:
Replace Catharanthus with Chrysanthemum 'Cloud Nine'.
Replace Verbena with Chrysanthemum 'Quaker'.
Replace each group of Antirrhinum 'Frontier Red' with nine Chrysanthemum 'Ruby Mound'.
Replace each group of Ageratum with five Chrysanthemum 'Pink Daisy'.
Fill in holes in border with Chrysanthemum 'Prom Queen'.

Concordance

One of the pleasures of talking to gardeners is all the bits of wisdom
and advice that they hand out. All these tips have the benefits of experience,
so I have passed them along here.

COLOR

Several wonderful books have been written about color (see Suggested Reading, page 135), to which I can add only a few notes. If you have red flowers and yellow flowers, and you want to keep them both but you don't like the way they clamor at each other, throw in a little orange and orange-yellow. Similarly, if you have strong magenta-pink (as in Lychnis coronaria) and chrome yellow, you can soften the impact with rose-pink and lavender. In the first case, you've just blended the colors the way you would paint; in the second, you've taken a strong color and tinted it with white, then added blue to create a hue that blends more softly with yellow. Understand that white flowers don't create smooth, soft transitions between other colors. If the linked two colors are pale tints, white flowers will blend them softly, but then, the pale shades would have blended even without white as an intermediary. Between two strong colors, white acts as a third strong color. For softness, instead of clumps of red, white, and blue in a row, try hues of pink and lavender placed between the red and blue.

CURATING THE COLLECTION

All the borders in this book are curated constantly, their owners moving or rejecting plants if they don't work out in a grouping, if they seem ill suited to the locale, or if the notion strikes that a plant would look absolutely wonderful somewhere else. Few specimens are excepted, unless moving them is a physical impossibility, and though most people keep notes, so that they could choose to wait until spring or fall to move plants, these gardeners shift things around with an impetuousness that can be alarming, especially when it is mid-July. Provided you're not moving something with a deep taproot, though, which you are unlikely to be able to dig up entirely, plants make intra-garden moves easily.

The key to success is understanding that a plant's roots are its intake system for water and nutrients; disrupt that system — either by breaking the roots or by exposing them to air — and a plant has to struggle to rebuild it. When a plant is dormant, during the winter, this is less of a problem, but root disturbance to a plant that is trying to support a crop of flowers or leaves can be a death knell, especially on a nice hot day when it really needs its water-delivery system. I've moved just about everything in our border at one time or another, from some Papaver orientale to some eight-foot Viburnum carlesii bushes (which took the aid of a backhoe), and both the perennials and the shrubs were on the brink of bloom. I've had complete success, which I attribute to transplanting in the evening, with cool, gray forecasts ahead; trying to scoop up as much of the rootball as possible; watering well immediately after the move, both to hydrate the plants and to eliminate any pockets of air around the roots; and watching the transplants if the weather becomes hot in the first week or so after the move. In one case, when a Macleaya cordata wilted terribly, I put up a little tent of burlap to protect it from the sun, mulched it, and kept the soil around it moist. (These plants are so robust as to be near-weeds in my border, so despite the fact that it has a deep and brittle root system, I moved it in late May, knowing that if it succumbed, there were many more that I could move in the fall.) In about ten days my specimen was fine.

GENERAL CULTIVATION

HOW CLOSE TO PLANT?

The consensus here is *very* closely. The reasons for this are that, first, it looks better — most gardeners abhor bare earth in their borders — and second, it really cuts down on weeding. A weed that is trying to get established in a crowded stand of desirable plants has to survive in dense shade and compete with a lot of greedy roots — so its chances are slim. In open ground, however, especially in all that good soil you've provided, weeds are winners — that's why they are called weeds. Caroline Burgess (see pages 98 – 105), who is responsible for Frank Cabot's garden, recommends tossing out your hoe, admonishing that if you can use it, your plants are too far apart.

WHEN TO CUT BACK, OR DOWN

The purpose of a border is to be beautiful, so the rule here is if a plant is no longer pretty to look at, cut it down. Most perennials will take this beautifully, and many, such as Alchemilla, Nepeta, Campanula, and Achillea, will respond by throwing out fresh new leaves, and often flowers. In any case, it's worth trying — the chances of killing something are negligible.

For bulbs, however, foliage is the conduit for energy that will provide for the following year's display — you'll have to put up with watching those leaves gradually yellow if you want next year's flowers. The best way to handle this is to grow something over the dying leaves or stalks. Gertrude Jekyll cut her delphiniums partway down and then redirected some nearby sweet peas (the perennial variety) to grow up them. The same could probably be done with lily stalks. Nasturtiums and any number of other vines would also suit this role. Miss Jekyll also used Gypsophila to cover the browning leaves of her Papaver orientale.

DIGGING UP AND DIVIDING

There are two reasons why gardeners dig up and divide clumps of perennials: one is to rejuvenate a clump that has begun to slack off in bloom; the other is to make many small plants from one large one. As a broad rule, lifting and dividing perennials every five to six years will suffice, and serves both goals. Many gardeners are in the habit of taking out an entire bed, digging in lots of manure or whatever other soil improver the bed requires, weeding both the soil and the clumps thoroughly, dividing the plants, and then replacing everything in the border. This can be done either in fall or in early spring, and the result is usually a wonderful surge of growth and blossoms, as well as a certain amount of extra plants to put elsewhere or to give away.

There are a few plants that are best left alone during such an overhaul (unless you are simply aiming to increase stock), as they will continue to grow larger and flower happily without division. Among these are peonies, Dictamnus, Baptisia (both of the latter have deep taproots, and so are next to impossible to dig up anyway), Dicentra, Platycodon, and Papaver orientale.

Some plants seem to need rejuvenating more often. Among these are irises, asters, and most Chrysanthemum species. Plants that tend to be invasive, such as Physostegia, are good subjects for frequent division, if for no other reason than to keep them in check. Apart from that, the consensus is that if you think something has gotten too large, dig it up and divide it, but otherwise leave it alone.

SELF-SOWN PLANTS

In the course of writing this book, one of the things I heard gardeners refer to with the most gratitude was the self-sown plant. These young plants are inevitably treasured, not only because they are gifts from nature, but because they always pop up in some completely unexpected place. Gardening requires that things be controlled, but the art of gardening lies in not constraining things too much. Self-sown flowers, along with plants that tumble beyond their bounds, are the perfect antidote to control. Among favorite self-sowers are Onopordum, Alcea rosea, and Digitalis — all biennials, which means you have to have a new crop coming along each year to ensure blossoms — and free-seeding perennials such as Campanula and Adenophora.

PLAGUES AND INSECTS

Few of the gardens in this book are ever sprayed with pesticides, fungicides, or herbicides, except in an extreme case, to nip a potentially devastating malady, such as iris borer, before it establishes itself and causes extensive damage. The pervading theory is that if you grow plants well, they don't succumb to bugs and diseases, and that the little bit the bugs do get can easily be spared. Growing plants well means growing plants that like your soil and climate, making your soil as good as you can make it, and being rigorous about the removal of dead wood and spent flowers.

PLANTS AND NOMENCLATURE

ANNUALS

An annual is a plant that goes through its entire life cycle in a single year, from sprouting of seed, through flowering and setting of new seed, to death. Many plants, however, are treated as annuals because they can be brought from seed to flower in a short time. Snapdragons, for example, though grown as annuals, are perennials. In my garden in New York City, snapdragons regularly survived the winter, turning into small, woody shrubs. *Hortus Third* indicates that in greenhouses, the common snapdragon, Antirrhinum majus, which is a Mediterranean native, will grow to six feet. Some true annuals are Centaurea cyanus (bachelor's-button), Petunia hybrids, Cosmos bipinnatus, and Lathyrus odoratus (sweet pea). Growers categorize plants that are generally grown as annuals with the terms *hardy*, *half-hardy*, and *tender*. These groupings refer to plants that will withstand varying amounts of frost, from some, to a little (with protection), to none at all.

BIENNIALS

Biennials are plants that complete their growing cycle in two years. In the first, they grow from seed to plant, but rarely flower. In the second, they flower, set seed, and die. Some familiar biennials are Alcea rosea (hollyhock), Digitalis purpurea (foxglove), most Verbascum species, and Campanula medium.

PERENNIALS

In botany, any plant that naturally survives more than two years is a perennial. Technically, then, trees and shrubs are perennials, but the term is commonly used to define herbaceous plants that are more enduring than their annual and biennial kin. *Herbaceous* derives from the botanical term "herb," which has nothing to do with culinary usefulness but defines any plant that is neither woody nor shrubby. The term "herbaceous perennial" is broadly used to describe any non-woody or non-shrubby plant that dies back to the ground with the onset of winter. It can be a confusing term, since many plants you'd expect to be in the group (the grasses are a good example) have leaves that survive winter quite beautifully. To be absolutely clear, and correct, stick to the botanical definitions: an herbaceous perennial is a plant that is neither tree nor shrub, but that naturally lasts more than two years.

SOIL AND ITS IMPROVEMENT

pH.

Expressed in terms of its pH, the relative acidity or alkalinity of soil runs from 3.5 (intensely acid) to 9.5 (intensely alkaline), with 7.0 being neutral. Most plants seem to prefer a neutral to slightly acid soil, and while most amateur gardeners probably couldn't tell you precisely where, numerically, their soil falls, they will certainly have a good idea of whether their soil is alkaline or acid, and to what degree. Simple testing kits are widely available.

ACIDITY

Most woodland plants prefer their soil on the acid side. These include rhododendrons, Kalmia (laurels), and azaleas, as well as perennial species such as Digitalis and Cimicifuga. Peat moss worked into the soil will generally increase its acidity, and there are fertilizers specially formulated for acid-loving plants.

LIME

A gardener who is limes the soil is reducing its acidity, or making it more alkaline. As some plants can't stand highly acid soil, you'll hear gardeners speak of liming specific plants to improve growth. Cynthia Clark (see pages 20 – 25) limes her Lavandula (she grows it in soil that is naturally sandy and very acid). *America's Garden Book* (James Bush-Brown and Louise Bush-Brown; Charles Scribner's Sons, New York, 1980) reports that Gypsophila, Anemone x hybrida, and the herbaceous species of Clematis, Dictamnus, and Delphinium prefer slightly alkaline soil. Lime comes either hydrated or as ground limestone.

FERTILIZERS

Gardeners refer to fertilizers with a set of three numbers, commonly "5-10-5" or "10-20-10." This is shorthand for the percentages of three critical mineral elements — nitrogen, phosphorus, and potassium — in the fertilizer's makeup. The reason that these three elements are so emphasized in fertilizers, even though calcium and magnesium are equally crucial to plant nutrition, is that the first three are known to be the ones most commonly deficient in cultivated soils. Every gardener has his or her pet fertilizer formula, and most of these have more to do with educated guesses, after observing the behavior of the plants in question, than with scientific soil testing. Although many gardeners never fertilize their borders, those who do generally recommend doing so just as the plants emerge in the spring, and again in early summer or midsummer. While annuals can be fertilized as late in the season as you wish, fertilizing perennials much after midsummer with a complete fertilizer is courting disaster in colder latitudes, because it might induce a lot of new, soft growth just when the plant should be retrenching for winter. It's true that granular fertilizers can burn foliage if incorrectly applied, but the commercially prepared bottles of water-soluble fertilizer that you put on the end of your garden hose virtually eliminate that risk. Generally, they can be sprayed on soil and foliage, even that of new transplants, without risk.

Gardeners are the only people you'll ever meet who discuss manure at a dinner party without blanching. As with fertilizers, most gardeners have their favorite kind. Manure is good for gardens not so much because it offers additional nutrition, but because it improves the soil's condition in much the same way an application of peat moss or leaf mold does: it adds organic matter (or humus) to the soil. Soil that is in good condition makes a plant's job of absorbing nutrients infinitely easier. Among the five most commonly available manures (cow, horse, pig, poultry, and sheep), poultry and sheep manures provide the greatest amount of nutrients. Several of the gardeners I interviewed swear by sheep manure, which has the most potassium of them all. As potassium is responsible for plant vigor, disease resistance, and root formation, gardeners who live near a shepherd may wish to partake.

MOISTURE

Generally speaking, the sandier your soil, the better drained it tends to be, but even in sandy soil, low-lying areas can be boggy. Conversely, clay soil tends to drain poorly. Gardeners who have heavy clay in their borders but want to grow a plant that prefers well-drained soil can do several things. One is to add sand and organic matter to improve the soil. Another is to raise the border, either by simply making the soil in it five to six inches higher than the ground around it — the plants in the border and a good mulching will prevent the soil from eroding — or by constructing some sort of solid edge around it, and raising it as high as several feet. In the latter case, whatever is containing the border should allow water to drain easily but shouldn't be so porous that soil can wash away. Another option is to install a drain several feet below ground level.

Gardeners with well-drained soil who want to grow a bog-loving plant, such as Japanese iris (Iris ensata), can sink a tub, with drainage holes a few inches up the side, into the border. Fill the tub with soil, and plant the bog-lover inside it. One caveat, however: though moisture will not seep out of the tub easily, it will also not seep easily *into* the tub. In a dry spell, the plant, whose roots are constrained to a small space, cannot benefit from a general watering. Remember to water it directly.

Suggested Reading

Color in My Garden by Louise Beebe Wilder. (Doubleday, Page & Co., 1918; reprinted by Atlantic Monthly Press, N.Y., 1990.) Read this book twice, first for the pleasure of Wilder's beautiful, descriptive prose, and then with a notebook in hand, for her invaluable advice. Written by an American gardener, for American gardeners, nothing you'll find in this book will set you up for disappointment — it is all very achievable. Especially useful is a chart at the end, listing, week by week, what plants were in bloom in her garden from May 1 through September 24.

Color in Your Garden by Penelope Hobhouse. (Little, Brown and Company, Boston, 1985.) The chapter in this book called "The Nature of Color" is the best analysis of color and how it works that I've ever found. If you have always thought that a scientific understanding of color would, for you, overburden the already complicated field of border design, read Hobhouse's explanation. You'll find that what seemed a confusing topic suddenly makes sense. Although some of the hardiness information is off, the rest of the book is a great source of ideas and inspiration.

Hortus Third, compiled by Liberty Hyde Bailey and Ethel Zoe Bailey. (Revised by the staff of the Bailey Hortorium, Cornell University. Macmillan Publishing Company, 1976.) *Hortus*, which is three inches thick and weighs a tremendous amount, is the American plantsman's bible. It is where to turn when you want to know exactly what a plant is, though it is limited to plants grown in the United States and Canada, including Puerto Rico and Hawaii. When you consider the scope of climatic conditions involved, however, this isn't much of a limitation.

The Illustrated Gertrude Jekyll. (Little, Brown and Company, Boston, 1988.) Reprint of Gertrude Jekyll's *Colour*

Schemes for the Flower Garden. (Longmans Green & Co., London, 1908.) This is the book that describes Jekyll's famous main border at her home, Munstead Wood, in Surrey. The new edition has planting plans of the border, and photographs to illustrate some of Jekyll's ideas about color. The text is the original, and in it you'll discover why the author became such a legend.

Perennials for American Gardens by Ruth Rogers Clausen and Nicolas E. Ekstrom. (Random House, N.Y., 1989.) This extremely useful book falls somewhere between *Hortus* and *Taylor's Guides* (see below). It has lots of color pictures (*Hortus* has none), indicates hardiness zones (another area where *Hortus* is weak), and covers more unusual varieties than *Taylor's Guides*.

Taylor's Guide to Perennials. (Houghton Mifflin Company, Boston, 1986.) This is a useful, quick cross-reference, with color photographs of just about every species in common use (415 photographs in all), plus descriptions, growing information, color and bloom-time charts, and much more. Although not comprehensive, it's still one of the best companions to take to the nursery. (Equally helpful are the guides to *Annuals and Bulbs.*)

Selected Sources

Sources for healthy plants are a border designer's lifeline. The first place to go for plants is always the local nursery (steer clear of outfits that have anything but vigorous plants displayed), but there are times when the plant you want isn't available locally. These are the mail order sources cited again and again as relaiable providers.

W. Atlee Burpee & Co.
300 Park Ave.
Warminster, PA 18974
Seeds. Everybody in this book uses them, and likes what they get.

Canyon Creek Nursery
3527 Dry Creek Rd.
Oroville, CA 95965
A good resource for uncommon perennials.

Carroll Gardens
P. O. Box 310
44 East Main St.
Westminster, MD 21157

Country Garden
P.O. Box 3539
Oakland, CA 94609
Seeds.
Cricklewood
11907 Nevers Rd.
Snohomish, WA 98290
Rare and unusual perennials.

Dutch Gardens
P. O. Box 200
Adelphia, NJ 07710
Great bulbs, great prices, plus a beautiful color catalog.

Hillside Gardens
Litchfield Rd.
P.O. Box 614
Norfolk, CT 06058
The nursery of American perennial guru Fred McGourty doesn't ship.

Holbrook Farm and Nursery
Rt. 2
Box 223B-1003
Fletcher, NC 28732
Perennials.

J. L. Hudson, Seedsman
P.O. Box 1058
Redwood City, CA 94064

P. de Jager and Sons
Box 100
Brewster, NY 10509
Bulbs.

Klehm Nursery
Rt. 5
197 Penny Rd.
South Barrington, IL 60010
Hostas, daylilies, irises, and peonies.

Matterhorn Nursery
227 Summit Park Rd.
Spring Valley, NY 10977
Perennials.

Montrose Nursery
P.O. Box 957
Hillsboro, NC 27278
Perennials.

Nabel's Nurseries
1485 Mamaroneck Ave.
White Plains, NY 10605
Does not ship, but offers a wide variety of stock, including unusual annuals.

Oliver Nursery
1159 Bronson Rd.
Fairfield, CT 06430
Does not ship, but the catalog is a valuable reference tool. They specialize in alpines, dwarf conifers, and other small-scale plants.

Park Seed Co.
Cokesbury Rd.
Greenwood, SC 29647-0001
Seeds, of course. The old, reliable source. Good quality, and a great, color-filled catalog.

Pickering Nurseries, Inc.
670 Kingston Rd.
Pickering, Ontario, Canada L1V 1A6
A favorite for roses.

Pierre Reath
100 Central Blvd.
Vulcan, MI 49892
Peonies.

Rice Creek Gardens
1315 66 Ave. NE
Minneapolis, MN 55432
Perennials.

Russell Garden
600 New Rd.
Churchville, PA 18966
Unusual perennials. Does not ship.

John Scheepers Inc.
RD 6, Phillipsburg Rd.
Middletown, NY 10940
Bulbs.

Schreiner's
3650 Quinaby Rd. N.E.
Salem, OR 97303
Irises.

Sunny Border Nurseries, Inc.
1709 Kensington Rd.
P.O. Box 86
Kensington, CT 06037
Wholesale only, but good for unusual perennials, e.g. Veronica longifolia 'Sunny Border Blue'.

Swan Island Dahlias
P.O. Box 700H
Canby, OR 97013

Thomson & Morgan
P. O. Box 1308
Jackson, NJ 08527
The seed source for all kinds of unheard-of and wonderful things.

André Viette Farm and Nursery
Rt. 1, Box 16
Fishersville, VA 22939
Perennials.

Wayside Gardens
1 Garden La.
Hodges, SC 29695-0001
Hardly a discovery, but Wayside is known to provide new and interesting varieties.

Gilbert H. Wild & Son, Inc.
787 Joplin St.
Sarcoxie, MO 64862-0338
Where everyone seems to turn for daylilies.

We-Du Nurseries
Rt. 5, Box 724
Marion, NC 28752
A favorite for perennials.

Woodlanders, Inc.
1128 Colleton Ave.
Aiken, SC 29801
Perennials.

Index